Righteous Prophet

ANDREW CHARLES PHINNEY

Welcome Righteous Prophets

SCAN ME

TABLE OF CONTENTS

ACKNOWLEDGEMENTS

Writing this book has been a journey filled with challenges, discoveries, and moments of pure divine inspiration. I could not have reached this point without the unwavering support, guidance, and love of so many remarkable individuals. Reflecting on this journey brings me immense joy and a profound sense of growth as a man of God in the prophetic.

To my wife, Roberta: thank you for standing by me through the late nights and long days spent locked away in my office or sitting in a coffee shop. Your patience and encouragement carried me through moments of doubt. You have always believed in me, never hesitating to support my dreams and calling. You consistently push me to see myself as God does. I wouldn't be where I am today without you. Your love and unwavering belief in me have made this dream a reality.

To Richard and Deb Cutsor: there are no words to fully convey what you both mean to my family. Your wisdom, guidance, and constructive critiques have shaped this book into what it is today. Your belief and support for my family and myself have given me the courage to keep pushing. Our conversations—filled with revelation and expertise—were invaluable to this process. I am deeply grateful for your contributions in proofreading and encouraging me to keep going, which continually reminded me why I wrote this book: to connect, to share, and to grow together.

To my mother, LuCinda: I am deeply grateful for the countless sacrifices you made for me throughout years of struggle and strife. Your resilience in seasons of lack, while raising us with strength and grace, is nothing short of inspiring. Thank you for always putting your children first, even when it cost you so much. Your prayers over the years are the reason I am here today. Words cannot fully express my gratitude for all you have done.

To my friend, Dr. Andy Kamerman: thank you for cheering me on with your enthusiasm and for listening to my countless ideas. Your faith in me has been a beacon of light and a source of confidence, encouraging me to pursue whatever God places on my heart. I am profoundly thankful for your friendship and honored to call you my brother.

Lastly, to everyone who inspired me, brought correction, or challenged me along the way—including those not named here but held close to my heart—thank you. This book exists because of you. I am honored that God divinely connected us, and I am profoundly grateful for your impact on this journey.

With deepest gratitude,

Andrew Phinney

FOREWORDS / ENDORSEMENTS

In every generation, God raises up voices to guide His people, call them to righteousness, and remind them of His divine plan. Righteous Prophet is a testament to the timeless truth that God's Word is alive and active, calling believers to walk in holiness and fulfill their divine purpose.

This book is more than a guide; it is a spiritual awakening, challenging readers to reflect on their lives and align with God's higher calling. With profound insights and passion, Andrew explores what it means to live as a righteous prophet—one who not only speaks the truth but embodies it in daily life.

With his exceptional understanding of Scripture, personal revelation, and practical wisdom, he leads us on a journey to discover the power of righteousness and the weight of prophetic responsibility.

In these pages, you will find encouragement, conviction, and a renewed understanding of God's desire for His people to live as vessels of His righteousness. Whether you are stepping into your prophetic calling or seeking a deeper walk with God, this book will inspire you to live boldly and faithfully in His presence.

Prepare your heart and mind to encounter the living God who still speaks through His righteous prophets today.

Jason Avanzini - *International Minister, John Avanzini Ministries*

The Prophet Amos proclaims, "Surely the Lord God does nothing Unless He reveals His secret counsel To His servants the prophets" (Amos 3:7, revealing the level of unique partnership God has set between himself and his oracles. There is undoubtedly a crucial need today for Prophets of God to take their place, yet this hour, like generations past, will require the Prophet to withstand and overcome the personal obscurities, wounding and attack that come with the territory of living as a mouthpiece for the Lord.

In his book, The Righteous Prophet, my friend Andrew Phinney serves the reader with a fresh perspective that will bring much healing and wholeness to Prophets and the prophetic movement alike. I am honored to endorse this book and believe it will not only be timely for many "budding" Prophets who are beginning their journey, but also timeless in its truths for those who are seasoned in the prophetic ministry. You will be blessed by this book!

Alex Parkinson - *International Evangelist, The Zion Company International*

In a world filled with devoted servants of Jesus, Andrew Phinney stands out as a true friend of the Lord. He leads from a place of deep communion with Christ, where Jesus consistently takes precedence in every aspect of his life and ministry. I believe Andrew represents a new generation of emerging leaders who prioritize the influence of Jesus above their own.

His prophetic ministry is characterized by creating spaces where people encounter the living Jesus and experience the transformative love of the Father. This book will not only challenge your understanding of prophetic ministry but also inspire and shape the way you lead your life, with Jesus firmly at the center.

Pablo Contreras - *Altar House Co | Bethel Leaders Network*

First of all, Andrew is family. From the kitchen table to the green room, from the sidewalk to the platform, the same honor, integrity, and prophetic mantle rest upon him. In Righteous Prophet, he doesn't just teach about the prophetic—he embodies it. This book is a powerful, much-needed guide that brings clarity, wisdom, and biblical solutions to the struggles prophets face. Andrew has a unique ability to illuminate the weight of the prophetic calling while equipping readers to carry it with strength, humility, and unwavering faith. If you are called to the prophetic, this is not just a book—it's a lifeline.

Bishop Jeff Coleman - *Jeff Coleman Ministries | New Harvest Church (Maryville, Tn.)*

I have been blessed by the knowledge and wisdom that flow throughout this amazing book. The statement in the first chapter of Andrew Phinney's book, Righteous Prophet, excited me. Andrew said, "The calling of a prophet is one of the most profound and sacred roles in the Christian faith. It is a mantle that carries great responsibility, requiring deep intimacy with God and a steadfast commitment to His will." The Lord told me years ago that, "all ministry flows out of the overflow of our personal relationship with our Lord Jesus."

Throughout the pages of this book, Andrew communicates the truth that our ability to be a vessel for Him to minister through must come from seeing God for who He is, seeing ourselves as God sees us, and seeing those we minister to as God sees them. The love of God is what makes the gifts in us palatable to others, and all spiritual gifts must be rooted and grounded in God's love. This is of utmost importance in all the five-fold ministry.

Andrew lays a wonderful foundation by explaining the difference between righteousness and holiness. He describes how understanding righteousness has profound implications for how we live prophetically. Andrew states, "It transforms how we see ourselves, how we see others, how we relate to God, and how we engage with the world."

Throughout this book, Andrew emphasizes that these truths are meant to be lived out in community. This message calls us to see people through God's eyes; otherwise, everything we hear or see prophetically will be distorted through our own perspective.

I believe that this book not only gives some clear direction on how to walk out the ministry of the prophet in every setting. It is dripping with the prophet reflecting the heart of God towards people. You will gain insight on how to respond to God's love, enjoy His love, and express His love to others. You will be equipped with some wonderful tools, which will be fueled by the love of God so that you may bear all your fruit in your season.

Pastor Tony Finley - *Senior Pastor of Faith Family Church | Third Year Pastor Class Teacher at Rhema Bible College | Regional Director for the Rhema Ministerial Association International (Omaha, Ne)*

Andrew is an articulate word smith with a passion for truth and insight, creating an authentic hunger in the reader to know God more deeply. Whatever Andrew undertakes carries the imprint of the Father's heart. He possesses wisdom beyond his years and hears God's voice with remarkable accuracy and clarity. I highly recommend this book.

Diane Cory - *Author of Christian Best Selling books - Born to Roar, Gotta Have God, God & Me | Host of "Children in Ministry Today" | 40+ years of trusted prophetic leader in various ministries*

One of the most confrontational subjects in the church today revolves around the conversation of the prophetic. Do Prophets still exist? Why do some denominations still advocate for them and others don't? How do you know whether or not someone is a true prophet? The harsh reality is, regardless of which side of the conversation you're on, both sides lack a biblical understanding of prophets and the purpose behind their assignment. In some instances, they've been reduced to fortune tellers. Others pursue them in hopes of receiving good news about what God is sending their way because of a current life struggle. In short, the entire gift of the five fold ministry has been perverted to satisfy personal gain, or dismissed by others because of the way it has been wrongly represented.

The good news is, prophets do exist. They are a vital part of the five fold function. To date, Ephesians 4 has yet to be accomplished in the body of Christ. The truth is, most people haven't been equipped. As a result, they don't edify, or build others up. Hence, we haven't come into the unity of the faith which is proof we haven't been perfected (we aren't mature).Our immaturity continues to toss us around causing us to embrace a multitude of doctrines, which are devised by the trickery of men (Ephesians 4: 11-16). Until the Body of Christ reaches a place of biblical maturity, five fold ministry remains necessary, which includes the operation and function of the prophet.

My good friend Andrew Phinney makes every effort to eliminate any confusion pertaining to this subject as he shares his life's experiences in Righteous Prophet. He provides a profound intimate view into the life of one who possesses the gift of a true prophet. The book offers a discerning perspective necessary for distinguishing the difference between that which is authentic, and that which is counterfeit. It reveals the characteristics and expectations of a true prophet to help identify this gift, to those who may be carrying it, but unaware they possess it.

One of the most difficult challenges we face today is seeing ourselves correctly. We have a tendency to let our failures, mistakes, or mishaps define us. However, who we are in the eyes of God is not determined by what we've been through. The prophet teaches us how to see what God sees when He looks at us. It is only when we learn to see ourselves correctly, we see others correctly. Why is this important? Because, people matter to God. When people don't matter to us, it's because we don't see them the way God sees them.

Whether we're willing to admit it or not, we need one another. We are designed for connection. (The whole body, joined, knit together by what every joint supplies Ephesians 4: 16).

This is the call of God that extends to every person on the planet. He's calling us to the unity of the faith and the knowledge of His Son, to become a perfect man - a perfect body - the Body of Christ! Without the prophet, we simply cannot   accomplish   this   task.

Bishop TC Holmes - *Lead Pastor Reformation Church | Ministry Leadership Training*

While the world constantly tries to redefine us and alter our values, this book is a powerful call to embrace our true Kingdom identity. With wisdom and clarity, Prophet Andrew Phinney will guide you to boldly step into the fullness of God's love and purpose for your life, and to count it all joy. Every page is a reminder that we are not just called —we are chosen, equipped, anointed, and appointed to make an impact for His glory. In a world that constantly tries to redefine us and alter our values, this book is a powerful call to embrace our true Kingdom identity. With wisdom and clarity, Prophet Andrew Phinney will guide you to boldly step into the fullness of God's love and purpose for your life, and to count it all joy. Every page is a reminder that we are not just called—we are chosen, equipped, anointed, and appointed to make an impact for His glory.

Dr. Dee Barker - *Coy & Dee Barker Ministries*

In a world that constantly tries to redefine us and alter our values, this book is a powerful call to embrace our true Kingdom identity. With wisdom and clarity, Prophet Andrew Phinney will guide you to boldly step into the fullness of God's love and purpose for your life, and to count it all joy. Every page is a reminder that we are not just called—we are chosen, equipped, anointed, and appointed to make an impact for His glory.n a world that constantly tries to redefine us and alter our values, this book is a powerful call to embrace our true Kingdom identity. With wisdom and clarity, Prophet Andrew Phinney will guide you to boldly step into the fullness of God's love and purpose for your life, and to count it all joy. Every page is a reminder that we are not just called—we are chosen, equipped, anointed, and appointed to make an impact for His glory.

Dr. Coy Barker - *Coy & Dee Barker Ministries*

INTRODUCTION

When I began to read "Righteous Prophet," I realized that this was going to be a comprehensive study that had been well thought out, prepared, and articulated by Prophet Andrew Phinney. Yes, Andrew has been a pastor and could easily function in that role, but as he and his wife have shared within this book —which I was privileged and blessed to read—those who know Andrew recognize that he has more than just the prophetic gift, he is indeed a prophet.

Now, let me add that since I personally know him, Andrew is not hung up on titles, nor is he interested in being labeled a prophet. However, the calling of a prophet gives Andrew credibility and credentials to write this prophetic instructional work and to share it with others who desire a more complete and balanced understanding of the role of a prophet in a church setting.

Righteous Prophet is written like a workbook, introducing deeper truths about what a prophet is and what a prophet isn't. Andrew takes his time in each chapter to honor and display certain biblical truths that are often ignored or overlooked in other published works about the prophetic ministry. The themes of edification, exhortation, and consolation are carefully unpacked in a neat and organized way—not with dry, dull substance, but with a life-giving, river-flowing energy that invites the reader to courageously jump in and begin to learn to swim in the prophetic waters.

At the same time, this book is penned like a novel, with one theme building upon another to bring sequential concepts together, creating a deeper understanding of the Kingdom values of prophetic ministry. The establishment of these foundational truths culminates in such a way that the reader will want to revisit the material again and again—because it is that good!

This book also serves as a manual, providing precise details on how a prophet should humbly serve in a church setting and how pastors can lovingly embrace them within the confines and oversight of the congregation. These are some of the most helpful suggestions and Kingdom attitudes I have ever seen written on the subject. They convey truths that establish harmony and unity rather than the often-present discontent and personal hurts that can arise between the pastoral gifting and the prophetic calling. This is highlighted well in Chapter 8 with the partial sentence, "Prophecy is a gift to serve others, not a measure of our worth." *Emphasis mine.*

Then, Chapter 6 begins to expand our thinking and previous teachings on the subject with its bold title: "What the Heck Is a Prophet, Anyways?" This is appropriately followed by a chapter simply labeled "Cracks." Cracks, if left untreated, can cause great harm within the body of Christ, and Andrew appropriately addresses the topic with grace, courage, and more grace—coupled with discipline mixed with gentleness —to aid in restoration, eliminate the enemy from gaining an unnecessary foothold, and honor Jesus in the process. Accountability is addressed with honesty and transparency, incorporating loving correction with encouragement and support. If followed, this honors God and impacts lives by reinforcing biblical standards that prevent cracks from reforming and causing further damage. What a great opportunity!

The personal struggles of a prophet are shared in depth, offering a deeper understanding of how fiercely the devil seeks to destroy the prophetic voice and why. Gaining insight into the weight prophetic people carry brings wisdom and knowledge rarely taught or shared, assisting pastoral leaders in their loving oversight of their flock. In Chapter 13, these words bring hope and joyful appreciation: the prophetic is not to be endured but cherished. Think about it—what would happen if all the gifts of God were cherished rather than attacked, argued against, or written about with strife and malice?

In Chapter 1, we read, "Prophetic ministry was never meant to operate under rigid human control. Its purpose is to reflect the heart and will of God, not human agendas or preference. When we limit it, we diminish its ability to bring about transformation, correction, and encouragement in the way God intends. Prophetic ministers need room to grow, yes, but also the freedom to fully express what God is saying—without compromise."

In conclusion, I suggest that this book is a must-read for every person, every library, every ministry, college, and seminary that desires to understand and fully embrace the ministry of a prophet and the gift of prophecy. There is a wealth of wisdom contained within these pages. Be prepared to underline, highlight, and apply these truths to your life. If you do so, you will be better equipped to understand and perhaps even flow in the prophetic in ways you once thought were only possible for others.

Jay W. West - *Revival and Conference Speaker | Author of Five Books | Host of "Directions" Television Program | United States National Prayer Council | Anointed 2 GO MdM*

CHAPTER ONE

------- ···••◈◈◈•••··· -------

HIRED GUN

------- ···••◈◈◈•••··· -------

A fter a full day of cross-country flights, I found myself in my hotel room, a blend of nerves and excitement swirling within me as I prepared to speak. God was speaking to my heart, but I couldn't shake the feeling of being out of my comfort zone. I was about to speak at a conference in the southern part of the country—a culture quite different from the churches I usually spoke to. They embraced the gifts and movement of the Spirit, but their expression was unfamiliar to me. They were a Word of Faith church at their core, with elements of charisma and revivalism. Their hunger for God was palpable—they were on fire, enthusiastic, and eager for the weeklong event ahead.

This gathering brought together renowned speakers from across the nation. These were individuals whose names you'd instantly recognize if you'd been a Christian for a few years. Some led massive movements, others had millions of Instagram followers, some were New York Times best-selling authors, and many hosted highly successful television programs. Then there was me—a relative unknown prophet who, though hidden by God, kept finding myself in rooms with influential people in the body of Christ. I didn't have a television show, a New York Times best-seller, or a multi-thousand-person church. My social media following was minuscule compared to theirs, and my name held little recognition within the American church.

I felt both confused and honored at the same time—humbled and eager, yet undeniably nervous.

The driver—a kind man who would later become a good friend—arrived to pick me up. We'd meet again over the years, as this conference became a recurring part of my life. As I climbed into his Chevy Traverse, he asked how I was feeling and what I planned to speak on. I confessed, "I'm not entirely sure why I'm here, but I'm excited and expectant to share what God has placed on my heart." He laughed, acknowledging that I was an odd fit—tattoos, flannel, skinny jeans, a flat-brimmed hat, and Jordans, heading to a church where suits and dresses were the norm. Then he said something that struck me: "If you don't even know why you're here, then God must be saying something important through you to us." Those words were the confirmation I'd been silently seeking from the Lord.

Arriving at the church, I was warmly welcomed in the green room by the leaders of the church and the other speakers. While I didn't know any of them other than the pastors of the church, who were very honoring and respectful, I imagined they were probably wondering the same thing as me: "What is this kid doing here, and who is he?" I was 10-20 years younger than all of the speakers, after all.

The service began, and the energy in the room was electric. When it was my turn to speak, I was introduced, and I stepped onto the stage. Though the setting was different, the experience felt familiar. As I delivered the message God had given me, His presence became tangible. People were visibly moved, and the sermon stirred a hunger for righteousness and intimacy with Christ. The altar time extended for hours as I prayed and prophesied over attendees. Their thirst for the prophetic was evident, but more importantly, they longed to hear the voice of the One who makes us righteous for themselves.

At conferences like this, it's common for ministers to leave for food or rest once the service switches from the sermon to ministering to the attendees, especially given the demands of multi-day events for the speakers. But to my surprise, when I returned to the green room with my driver—who also doubled as my armor bearer—all the speakers were still there, waiting.

Entering the room, I was met with an unexpected sight. Each person, one by one, approached me with heartfelt words of encouragement. They shook my hand, hugged me, and offered sincere compliments on the message I'd shared. One well-known figure, deeply respected in Christian circles, told me the sermon had transformed their ministry—a humbling sentiment from someone with nearly three decades of experience.

Then came the final encounter. A man I didn't know at the time—but have since come to know well—approached me. His vibrant, multicolored outfit, gold glasses, and bold jewelry made him impossible to miss. Towering over me, he placed his hands firmly on my shoulders, his powerful voice resonating as he leaned in close. "Son," he said, "words can't express what I saw on you today. All I can say is this: Don't let anyone misuse the voice God has given you. Protect it with everything you have."

With that, he moved aside, took his wife's hand, and left the room without further explanation, a smile, or even a goodbye. His words pierced my heart, reshaping my perspective on ministry and leaving an indelible mark on my life.

That moment forever altered my ministry. It reminded me of the weight of the calling God had placed on my life and the importance of stewarding it with integrity. While I may have felt like an outsider walking into that conference, God used the experience to confirm that He had a purpose for my voice—a purpose worth protecting at all costs. That it was going to be used outside of my stream, and that He would use me wherever He chose, outside of my understanding.

I hope that all prophets and those with prophetic callings can learn from the encounter I had with a man who has been in ministry for over 40 years. My journey has not been without its challenges. I've experienced hurt and have often felt like a workhorse in ministry. Many loved the gift God entrusted me with, even if they didn't necessarily care for me as a person. The undeniable accuracy of prophetic words, the "reading of their mail," and the miracles that followed made the gift evident. Unfortunately, some people used this gift for their personal or ministry gain, without regard for me as a man or a child of God.

Without a national platform or recognition, I found myself being used for the gift and then set aside. I've always prided myself on serving without expectations and maintaining an undeniable work ethic, but many saw this and took advantage. Most of the time, it wasn't out of malice—it just seemed to happen again and again.

It often felt as though people wanted me to serve and work for their ministries but then be pushed aside until my gifting was needed again. Once, a fellow leader told me I didn't fit their "culture," but they loved my gift and would call when they needed me to preach or minister prophetically. They encouraged me to pursue what I felt God was calling me to do and reassured me I wasn't bound to their network or its requirements. While it was freeing in some ways, it also felt like an indirect rejection—like I was being asked to sit at the kids' table until it was time for the adults to call me up for entertainment or ministry.

Eventually, I was told I could—and should—protect the gift God gave me to steward. That revelation was transformative. I realized I could say no. For so long, I had accepted being dishonored and disrespected, patiently waiting for opportunities to serve the body of Christ, even in the face of mistreatment.

But here's the truth: I don't hold any resentment toward those people or ministers. I've come to see that, at the time, I didn't fully understand my own purpose or gifting. How could I expect others to honor and support what I hadn't yet grasped? I likely didn't communicate my worth, my development, or my needs in a way that would have helped them guide me in those early stages of ministry.

I've also come to understand that I am a unique individual, and that can make it challenging for others to know how to support me. Looking back, I see grace in those moments— even the difficult ones. They've shaped me into who I am today—a person with deeper understanding, purpose, and confidence in what God has called me to do. This is why I am writing this book. I want to help the unhelpable and the unseen in our prophetic culture. I want to remind and affirm that we are valuable members of the body of Christ with so much purpose. People don't understand us because they don't first understand themselves through the mind of

Christ and the thoughts God had for us long before we were woven into our mothers' wombs. So, after receiving this word to protect my voice and the gift God gave me—because people would try to use and abuse it—I wanted scripture to back up this life-changing revelation. God led me to 1 Kings 22.

In this passage, King Ahab is seeking guidance on whether he should attack Ramoth Gilead. He wants to know if God will back him. Ahab has 400 prophets who are prophesying victory, telling him that God will deliver him a win. King Ahab discusses the matter with Jehoshaphat, King of Judah, seeking his support. Jehoshaphat says, "My people are your people." Ahab advises him to seek the Lord's will on the matter.

I stopped here when I first read this. I was confused. How could the deceived king give such wise counsel? The answer is that Ahab had created a group of "prophets"—but more accurately, false prophets—who were there to speak only what the king wanted to hear. They prophesied only good things about him and his plans. These "prophets" were hired to speak what Ahab wanted, to tickle his ears and make him feel good. Ahab had been deceived into thinking these men spoke for God, but in reality, they were just hired voices. They weren't authentic prophets—they were hired prophets.

Ahab says that there is only one voice in the land who speaks the word of the Lord, and that is Micaiah, the son of Imlah. Ahab admits he hates him because Micaiah never speaks anything positive about him. Jehoshaphat urges Ahab not to speak so harshly, as Micaiah is a true prophet of the Lord. So they send for Micaiah, asking him what God thinks of the matter.

The people sent to get Micaiah try to prepare him, saying, "Look, all the other prophets are predicting success for the king. Let your word agree with theirs, and speak favorably."

Micaiah responds, "As surely as the Lord lives, I can tell him only what the Lord tells me."

When Ahab asks Micaiah what the Lord says about their attack, Micaiah answers sarcastically, "Attack and be victorious, for the Lord will give it into the king's hand."

Ahab replies, "How many times must I make you swear to tell me nothing but the truth in the name of the Lord?"

Micaiah then says, "I saw all Israel scattered on the hills like sheep without a shepherd, and the Lord said, 'These people have no master. Let each one go home in peace.'"

Micaiah continues, prophesying Ahab's death and the demise of his kingdom. Ahab throws Micaiah in prison for speaking against him. Ultimately, what Micaiah prophesied comes true: Ahab is killed in battle, and all that he built is destroyed.

There's so much to unpack here, but I want to focus on Micaiah's decision to speak only what the Lord instructed, despite King Ahab's desire for a more convenient message. In prophetic ministry, there's often a desire for the gift— but only if it conforms to certain expectations or looks a particular way.

To be clear, I'm not advocating for words of doom, gloom, or fire-and-brimstone declarations. That's not the purpose or calling of prophetic ministry. However, prophetic ministry is entrusted to people who must be biblically literate and uncompromising in speaking only what the Lord reveals. Prophets cannot—and should not—be told what to minister, how to minister, or confined to pre-determined parameters. To do so handcuffs God from ministering in the way He chooses and rejects the unique design and purpose He has placed on His prophetic people.

Now, I can already sense the concerns of pastors and leaders rising to the surface, and I understand them. Yes, there's absolutely a place for establishing guardrails to help developing prophetic ministers grow and minister safely—

for themselves and the people they serve. I agree with that. But if those guardrails are maintained solely to confine prophetic ministry to a specific box, it becomes harmful— not only to the prophetic minister but also to the broader culture and body of Christ.

Prophetic ministry was never meant to operate under rigid human control. Its purpose is to reflect the heart and will of God, not human agendas or preferences. When we limit it, we diminish its ability to bring about transformation, correction, and encouragement in the way God intends. Prophetic ministers need room to grow, yes, but also the freedom to fully express what God is saying—without compromise.

Leaders and pastors, I want to take a moment to speak to you. First, let me say how much I deeply appreciate your hearts, your dedication, and your love for God's people. Your commitment to shepherding the flock is invaluable.

I want to encourage you: It's okay for prophetic ministry to get a little messy or for people to occasionally miss it. Just as you are learning and growing in your role, so are we. Mistakes happen. But trying to prevent any potential mess by avoiding prophetic ministry altogether is like stopping a child from riding a bike because they might fall and scrape their knee. Growth requires practice, and practice often comes with a little mess. Let us prophetic people scrape a knee every once in a while.

People need a safe environment to learn, grow, and even make mistakes. They also need guidance to clean up the mess and take valuable lessons from it. Without those experiences, there's no room for growth, no development of character, and no expansion of their gifting. As Proverbs reminds us, "Where there are no oxen, the manger is clean." But it's through the work—and yes, the occasional mess—that real fruit is produced.

So, I urge you not to keep prophetic people out of your ministries out of fear of a mess. The mess can be a powerful teacher. Thank you for your willingness to embrace the prophetic gift and the people who carry it. Your devotion to the body of Christ and its growth is seen and appreciated.

I'm personally so thankful for the pastors in my life, both past and present. They've shaped me in countless ways, even those who mishandled me. In fact, I might be most thankful for the ones who didn't get it right, because those experiences taught me some of the most important lessons. Thank you for your hearts, your leadership, and your willingness to walk alongside all of us in this journey.

PREFACE

The following four chapters may appear fundamental to some, and indeed, they are foundational principles. However, I am of deep conviction that these biblical teachings are essential for both those in the office of the prophet and individuals operating in prophetic ministry. Gaining a deep revelation of these truths is crucial for maintaining a healthy, accurate, and pure prophetic calling.

I encourage you to approach these next four chapters with an open heart, allowing the Lord to guide and affirm your understanding. Seek His wisdom to reveal any areas of unbelief or places where your perspective may need realignment. As you engage with these foundational teachings, may they prepare you for the deeper exploration of prophetic ministry that are filled in the chapters following.

-Andrew Phinney

CHAPTER TWO

RIGHTEOUSNESS THROUGH JESUS: FOUNDATION OF THE PROPHET

There seems to be a word that echoes from the mountaintops of our pulpits and whispers quietly in the corners of the church simultaneously. It has been preached and emphasized for hundreds, if not thousands, of years. Yet, there remains a significant misunderstanding surrounding this word; perhaps we have even misdefined it. The body of Christ has often found itself held at gunpoint because of this misunderstanding, as the world wields it against us as a weapon. This word has fueled wars and won hearts throughout the annals of history.

As it resurfaces with increasing frequency, I would even call it a buzzword today. I became acutely aware of its significance when God inspired the title of this book, and as I write these very words, I feel its weight. My aim is not to simply attract attention but to bring clarity and revelation that empowers you in your divinely appointed calling. So, let's dive deeper into this vital concept!

The word I'm speaking of is righteousness. From my perspective, righteousness is perhaps the most important gift that Jesus paid for on the cross. That may sound like a bold and controversial statement, so allow me to elaborate.

At its core, righteousness can be defined as being in right standing with our Heavenly Father. This state is achieved solely through Jesus Christ and not by our own deeds or works (2 Corinthians 5:21). Righteousness flows from Jesus' sacrifice on the cross, His resurrection, and His current position seated at the right hand of the Father. The Bible affirms that we, too, are seated in heavenly places with Christ (Ephesians 2:6). This profound truth illustrates that the gates of heaven are wide open to all humanity, offering us the free will to choose a relationship with God. This fulfills God's original purpose for creating us: to be in intimate relationship with Him. Such intimacy can only be achieved through, by, and in Jesus (Romans 5:19). Jesus, being fully God and fully man (John 1:14; 1 Timothy 2:5; Philippians 2:7; Colossians 2:9; Hebrews 4:15; John 10:30; Romans 8:3; Hebrews 2:17; Galatians 4:4-5; Philippians 2:5-11), is the only way this righteousness is made accessible to us.

Before moving forward, we must understand the distinction between righteousness and holiness. Often, people confuse these two terms, but they serve different roles in our spiritual journey. Righteousness pertains to our standing before God—our identity in Christ—while holiness refers to our behavior and how we live out that identity.

To fully embrace righteousness, we need more than mere intellectual understanding; it must become heart knowledge. When righteousness transforms from a theological concept into a foundational aspect of our identity, we begin to live from it rather than striving to achieve it. This shift is crucial for living a life that is both abundant and aligned with God's will.

This is what is meant by "the experiential Gospel." It's not something we merely know or strive to keep up with—it's something we experience and seek out. The things of the kingdom of God must be experienced, not just studied. While gaining as much studied revelation as possible is important, it cannot remain theory; it must become reality.

You might ask, "How can I embrace righteousness while living in a fallen world?" or "How can I experience righteousness when my life feels like it is under constant attack?" Perhaps you question how to live from a place of righteousness when so much of what you were taught in church seems to contradict this concept. Many of us have been taught to modify our behavior in an effort to avoid sin and stay holy.

I wrestled with these questions as well when I first encountered the idea of righteousness as a kingdom principle. When I began to seek the Scriptures on righteousness, it felt like tapping into a small leak in a dam. Suddenly, the floodgates opened. I discovered that righteousness is a foundational aspect of the kingdom because it is who Jesus is.

If Jesus is the cornerstone of our faith, it logically follows that righteousness is integral to the foundation of the kingdom. If our righteousness is indeed through Christ, as Romans articulates, it connects a multitude of questions I've had since becoming a follower of Jesus. Let's explore a few of those questions briefly—they could easily warrant a separate book in themselves.

1. How Can We Be Righteous If We Are Sinful?

The answer to this question has already been covered, but it bears repeating. Righteousness comes through Jesus—it is not something we strive to achieve but rather something we are. Through salvation, we are brought into the New Covenant and gifted with righteousness. Sin is no longer part of our true nature; it has been moved outside of us as we have been given the divine nature of God (2 Peter 1:4). In salvation, we became a new creation—a gift Jesus freely gave us through His sacrifice on the cross.

It's like receiving Jesus' perfect report card in exchange for our own, which was filled with F's. When we step into the gift of salvation, we are clothed in His righteousness. Thus, the question itself becomes invalid because righteousness is not based on our actions but on Jesus' actions.

Holiness, however, is connected to our actions. A more accurate question might be: "How can we, as followers of Jesus, be holy if we still sin?" (See the next chapter on holiness for the answer.)

2. If We Are Grafted Into the Vine with God as the Root, Does That Make God Sinful If We Are Attached to Him?

This was an honest question I asked God during my exploration of righteousness. It was a significant point of confusion for me, and I needed clarity before I could fully embrace the concept. What I discovered is this: sin no longer dwells within us once the old self is dead and we are made new. I wish the church could grasp the depth of what "new" truly means. This word is monumental. It signifies something so unprecedented that there is nothing like it in the cosmos—never has been, and never will be. WOW. That realization completely shifted my understanding of righteousness.

If we are made that unique and in God's image (Genesis 1:27), it means our uniqueness is tied to our calling and purpose. It means we play a vital role in God's family because no one else can bring what we bring to the table. The answer, then, is a resounding YES!

3. How Is It Possible for Jesus to Return for a Spotless Bride When I Am Not Spotless Myself?

This question weighed heavily on me for years—from the day I got saved until just a few years ago. I used to believe that the Bride of Christ had to be a perfect, utopian collective of Christians living in flawless unity. Over time, it became clear this wasn't realistic—not with the state of the world, the body of Christ as a whole, or my own imperfections.

However, understanding that through salvation we are made new creations, and that righteousness is a gift given by Jesus, changed everything. We are not made righteous by our actions but by receiving righteousness through Jesus.

What once seemed like an impossible ideal became a simple, foundational truth rooted in the Gospel. Now, whenever I read Scripture about righteousness, I see it as our new identity in Jesus. He has made us righteous.

To fully understand righteousness, we must return to the cross—the pivotal point of our faith. It was at the cross that righteousness was reintroduced to the world. When Adam and Eve succumbed to deception, sin entered and disrupted the intimate connection humanity had with God. Righteousness was obscured by shame and condemnation, marking humanity's first encounter with the darkness of a fallen world.

In that moment, Adam and Eve accepted the enemy's lie, forfeiting their divine inheritance. The gift of righteousness was hidden behind that lie until Jesus came to pull the veil away. While a few individuals throughout history maintained intimacy with God, most of humanity lived in deception and brokenness, forfeiting the gift of righteousness.

At the cross, Jesus unveiled the righteousness that had been shrouded in darkness. By paying the ultimate price to conquer sin, He established a new covenant between Himself and the Father—a covenant we partake in through Him.

Understanding righteousness has profound implications for every aspect of our lives. It transforms how we see ourselves, others, and our relationship with God. It changes how we engage with the world. If I view myself as distant from God, it becomes challenging to hear His voice because I assume He's far away or that I am too insignificant to matter to Him.

When we live from the truth of our righteousness in Christ, we walk in closer communion with Him and fully embrace the identity He has given us.

But when I begin to see myself as God sees me, hearing His voice becomes natural. He is as close as a friend and, like a loving Father, delights in speaking to His children— willing to drop everything to spend time with them. Understanding that God is not distant and loves His children unconditionally makes it easier to see why He loves those around me, even strangers. His love for them is just as real as His love for me.

Righteousness is not merely something we receive at salvation to feel superior to others who have not yet accepted Christ as Lord and Savior. Moving from sinner to saint does not grant us a "get out of jail free" card. Instead, it calls us to live from the gift of righteousness, seeing the world through Christ's lens. This perspective allows us to view people not as they are, but as they were created to be.

Such a mindset propels us toward the incredible things God has planned for us while glorifying Him along the way. It also draws others closer to His Kingdom.

Here are two key points to understand about righteousness before exploring the prophetic and prophets:

1. Righteousness is Our Identity

When we accept Jesus as Lord and Savior, we receive a new identity. We are no longer defined by past mistakes, sins, or shortcomings but by our relationship with Christ. This identity as the righteous is not just a title; it is a transformative reality that shapes the way we live.

In 2 Corinthians 5:17, it says, "if anyone is in Christ, he is a new creation; old things have passed away; behold, all things have become new." This transformation shifts our identity from sinner to saint, from condemned to righteous.

2. Righteousness Empowers Us for Service

Righteousness is more than a status; it is a source of empowerment. Understanding that we are righteous through Christ equips us to serve others confidently, especially in a world filled with strife, injustice, and suffering.

Acting from a place of righteousness allows us to become agents of change. Our actions can reflect God's love and grace, drawing others to experience His goodness. As the light of the world and the salt of the earth (Matthew 5:13-16), we are equipped by this understanding to fulfill our calling.

Righteousness also fosters intimacy with God. Through Jesus, we have direct access to the Father. Hebrews 4:16 invites us to "approach God's throne of grace with confidence." We can come before Him without fear or shame, knowing we are accepted and loved as His children.

When we grasp our righteousness, our prayer life deepens, our worship becomes more genuine, and our relationship with God thrives. We no longer bear the weight of our shortcomings but instead lean into His grace, confident in our standing before Him. Rather than running from God when we sin, we run toward Him. He has cleansed us of shame and imparted peace through His nature, which He graciously shares with us.

Even with this knowledge in our hearts, living out righteousness can be challenging, especially in a fallen world filled with trials. Yet, it is in these challenges that our understanding of righteousness becomes vital. It sustains us even when life seems to overwhelm us.

Many struggle with the concept of generational curses—patterns of sin and dysfunction passed down through families. While these ideas may arise from Old Testament beliefs, they do not define our identity in Christ. Let me clarify: you are either part of a bloodline bound by generational sin, or you are made new in Christ, adopted into a new family (Ephesians 1:5) with the most amazing

Heavenly Father. Accepting Jesus breaks the cycle of sin that may have bound our families.

As new creations, we are not only dead to our old selves but also given a new lineage and bloodline. Our connection is no longer tied to our earthly family but to God Himself through Christ's blood. Having been buried and raised with Christ and now seated in heavenly places (Romans 6:4-5), it becomes impossible to be bound by generational curses.

Let me explain what "curse" means biblically. The word "curse" in Scripture often refers to taking someone or something lightly or undervaluing them. This understanding shifts perspective. When we curse others—whether sinners or believers—we devalue them, seeing them as less than who God created them to be.

Furthermore, cursing others or ourselves means entertaining thoughts about them that God does not have. It aligns us with the enemy's view rather than God's. This realization is profound. Moving forward, especially in prophetic ministry, we must honor others—recognizing their true worth—instead of cursing them.

Finally, in Christ, we have the authority to declare freedom over ourselves and those we encounter. Galatians 3:13 states, "Christ redeemed us from the curse of the law by becoming a curse for us." This means that any curse spoken over us or negative belief we have held about ourselves can be broken through the righteousness we have in Christ.

Each of us faces personal battles—addictions, doubts, fears, and insecurities. In these struggles, it is crucial to remember that our righteousness does not depend on our performance but on Christ's sacrifice. When we stumble, instead of wallowing in shame, we can approach God with a repentant heart, confident in His grace to restore us. This understanding propels us forward, enabling us to live from our righteous identity rather than striving for it.

Righteousness is not solely an individual experience; it is meant to be lived out in community. The body of Christ is called to support and uplift one another in the journey of faith. This is particularly significant for prophetic people.

Encouraging One Another

As members of the body of Christ, we are called to encourage one another in righteousness—celebrating victories, supporting each other through struggles, and reminding one another of our identity in Christ.

When we gather in fellowship, we create an environment where living out the righteousness of Christ becomes a shared reality. Hebrews 10:24-25 exhorts us to "consider how we may spur one another on toward love and good deeds, not giving up meeting together, as some are in the habit of doing, but encouraging one another." A community rooted in righteousness strengthens the understanding and practice of our identity in Christ.

When the church embodies righteousness, it becomes a beacon of hope in the world. A community grounded in righteousness reflects God's love, grace, and truth—not by achieving but by believing. When we live from faith in what Christ has done, the world around us begins to change.

In a society rife with division and strife, the church has a unique opportunity to model reconciliation and unity. By living out our identity as the righteous ones, we can demonstrate the transformative power of the gospel, inviting others to experience God's love.

As we reflect on righteousness through Jesus, we are called to embrace this foundational truth in our lives. Righteousness is not merely a theological concept; it is our identity, our empowerment for service, and our gateway to intimacy with God.

In a world that often misunderstands and misrepresents righteousness, we have the opportunity to redefine it through our lives. By embodying righteousness, we become agents of change, bringing hope and healing to those around us.

Let us commit to a life marked by righteousness, recognizing it as a gift freely given through Jesus Christ. In doing so, we unlock a deeper relationship with God and a more authentic expression of our faith. As we navigate life's complexities, may we always return to the truth of our righteousness in Christ, allowing it to shape our identities and transform our communities for His glory.

Righteousness is not just a doctrine; it is the essence of our lives in Christ—the cornerstone of our faith and the divine inheritance that empowers us to live fully in our calling, especially in the prophetic. This understanding equips us to navigate a fallen world, rooted in our identity as God's righteous ones, drawing others into the transformative love of Jesus.

As you journey through this understanding of righteousness for prophets, I encourage you to dive into the Scriptures, pray for revelation, and allow the Holy Spirit to guide you. Live from a place of righteousness, and watch as it transforms your life and those around you. Embrace the fullness of what it means to be in right standing with God, letting that truth resonate in every aspect of your life.

In a time when righteousness is often misunderstood, let us be ambassadors of Christ's love, shining brightly in a world that desperately needs it. May we walk boldly in our identity, knowing we are His righteousness—called to reflect His glory and bring His kingdom to earth.

CHAPTER THREE

HOLINESS VS RIGHTEOUSNESS

Now that we understand the gift of righteousness through Jesus, we must address another often misunderstood concept: holiness. I believe that we have muddled the definition of holiness. In most teachings on the topic, it is often explained as an offshoot of righteousness, but they are very different.

Let us define righteousness in the simplest way so we can distinguish it from holiness. Righteousness is being in right standing with our Heavenly Father. As we defined earlier, righteousness is not achieved but received through Jesus. It is a gift granted to us through the bloodline of Jesus, into which we are grafted. Our relationship with Christ is not even a defining factor. The only thing holding us or others back from righteousness through Jesus is knowing and receiving the gift freely. It has always been available to everyone; it simply depends on whether one accepts and receives it.

Now, let us shift gears to define holiness and clearly differentiate between these two core pieces of our faith. Holiness can be defined as being set apart, pure, and dedicated to God, both in character and conduct. In the Bible, holiness is deeply associated with God's nature and is an essential attribute of His being. It involves moral purity, spiritual integrity, and a commitment to living according to God's standards. Holiness involves turning away from sin and living in a way that reflects God's righteous and pure character (Leviticus 19:2; 1 Peter 1:15-16).

What happens, then, when we do sin? Does that make us unholy? Let us take a moment to thank Jesus for dying on the cross, paying for our sins, so we can come to Him with repentant hearts and be washed clean. This can be difficult for people to understand, but as prophetic individuals, we must be able to think in multiple realms. We need to view things both from an earthly perspective and a heavenly perspective.

From an earthly realm view, we need to come to God and repent with humble hearts. This is crucial. This is often where we lose people because discussions about righteousness and holiness sometimes neglect repentance. However, they are all interconnected. A person living from righteousness should be so driven to run to the Father and communicate with Him in repentance, instead of hiding in shame or guilt over shortcomings. This aligns with the holiness we are set apart for.

Simultaneously, from the heavenly perspective, we need to see biblical foundations as existing outside time. Holiness has been paid for, so we are set apart as a holy body—sinless, blameless, and pure. This is somewhat hard to grasp at times, but Scripture assures us that we are seated in heavenly places (Ephesians 2:6). It doesn't say we are going to be; it says we are. Both perspectives—the earthly and the heavenly—are valid and essential.

Holiness means being dedicated or consecrated to God, separated from the world and its influences (Romans 12:1-2). This applies to people, places, or objects, all of which can be deemed "holy" when set apart for God's purposes. God's holiness is absolute and unchangeable. He is completely righteous, morally perfect, and distinct from all creation (Isaiah 6:3; Revelation 4:8). The holiness of God is who He is, and as His image-bearers, we are called to reflect His holiness in our lives.

Holiness and sanctification go hand in hand. They are like peanut butter and jelly. Peanut butter is good on its own, and jelly is good on its own, but together they make complete sense. Sanctification means being set apart from the world as a holy child of God for His purposes.

Sanctification could be an entire book in itself, as debates abound within the body of Christ. Some argue that sanctification occurs at salvation; others say it is progressive throughout life, or that it happens fully in heaven. All these perspectives can be justified if we isolate certain Scriptures. However, to fully understand sanctification, we must examine the Bible as a whole, considering historical and linguistic contexts in both Greek and Hebrew.

After studying these theories, I lean toward the belief that we are sanctified at salvation, and as we live from Christ's righteousness, we grow in awareness of the sanctification that Jesus has paid for. Holiness is the actions we choose based on our revelation of being sanctified through Christ as righteous. Holiness is not just an inward state; it is expressed outwardly through loving others, pursuing justice, and living righteously (Micah 6:8; Ephesians 4:24).

In summary, biblical holiness is living in purity, obedience, and devotion to God. It reflects His character and demonstrates our being set apart for His divine purposes. As prophets and prophetic people, we need to not just be biblically literate in righteousness but also walk a life of biblical holiness.

CHAPTER FOUR

─────── ⬥ ───────

UNTOLD SECRETS OF THE
PROPHETIC

─────── ⬥ ───────

Over the years, I've collected countless books on the prophetic and attended numerous conferences—enough that it feels like I could have a PhD in prophecy by now. Yet, I am constantly discovering new depths within the prophetic heart of God. I've invested a great deal of time studying this incredible spiritual gift that the Holy Spirit has graciously given to the body of Christ. Through this journey, I've grown to deeply love both the prophetic community and the gift itself.

This chapter will not focus on how to prophesy or provide tips on prophecy. There are already many excellent resources available, such as You May All Prophesy by Steve Thompson and Basics of the Prophetic by Kris Vallotton, to name just a couple among the hundreds of great options.

However, one aspect I wish was emphasized more frequently, even before learning the basics of prophecy, is the importance of seeing people through God's eyes. It is essential to understand, biblically, what God says and thinks about people. Without this foundational understanding in our hearts, we risk delivering prophetic words filtered through our own judgments, which can distort their accuracy and impact.

It doesn't matter whether the word is for a world government, a global leader, your elderly neighbor, a homeless man, or even a church you disagree with—before stepping into prophetic ministry, we must know what God thinks about people. Everything we perceive or communicate prophetically is filtered through our own perspectives. Therefore, it's critical that our lens is clear and pure. As Jesus says in Matthew 7:3-4, "Why do you look at the speck in your brother's eye, but do not notice the log in your own eye? Or how can you say to your brother, 'Let me take the speck out of your eye,' when there is a log in your own eye?"

We often interpret this passage as a call to repentance or as a warning against judging others—both valid perspectives. However, I'd like to offer another interpretation.

What if this passage is also teaching us not to give prophetic words without first having a clear understanding of who someone is and what they were created for? What if it is a caution against speaking into people's lives with judgment in our hearts? Could the imagery of logs and specks be a reminder to focus on God's grace in others' lives instead of highlighting their flaws? (Grace being the empowerment to do the will of God.)

What if we instead honored the image of God within each person, loving them through the prophetic, and casting out all fear by shining God's love and light on them?

What if we prophesied from a lens that reflects God's perspective—seeing people as He sees them?

Consider the truth that the righteousness of Christ is for all people—both sinners and saints. Even though a sinner may not yet have received Christ as Lord and Savior, the gift of righteousness is available to them; it simply has not been revealed or accepted yet, which only happens through salvation. As saints, however, we know of this righteousness because we have been crucified, buried, and resurrected with Christ (Romans 6:3-7). Why not adopt this lens as the foundation from which we prophesy? This simple yet profound revelation changed everything for me. It is the greatest thing God has graciously taught me, and it must be foundational for us, especially as we navigate the challenges the world is facing.

Before we delve further into the Untold Secrets of the Prophetic, there are a few foundational Scriptures that we must fully grasp. Genesis 1:26 says, "Let us make man in our image, after our likeness." The word "image" signifies that God sculpted us to reflect His nature, like a mirror.

This means we carry immense value—so much so that Jesus paid the ultimate price on the cross for us. If we, as individuals, are of such extraordinary worth to God, then so is every other person He created. Jeremiah 1:5 tells us, "Before I formed you in the womb, I knew you," demonstrating the deep love and value God places on each person.

To prophesy effectively, we must adopt this perspective of God's love for His creation. Equally important is understanding God's love for us. These two truths—how God sees people and how He loves us—are deeply interconnected. Approaching prophecy with this understanding allows us to grow in this gift in a healthy and impactful way.

While these truths are foundational, there are key elements of prophetic ministry that are often overlooked. Let's explore a few of these.

- ***The Command to "Desire Prophecy"***

When Paul writes in First Corinthians 14:1, "Earnestly desire the gift of prophecy," it serves as a powerful call to pursue, study, and grow in this gift. This verse is commonly referenced in prophetic circles, and rightly so. However, let's break down verses 1-5 to explore their deeper meaning.

Verse 1 begins, "Pursue love, yet..." The word "yet" has caused confusion for some, leading them to prioritize prophecy over love. However, the Greek word here can also be translated as "and," which provides a clearer reading: "Pursue love, and also earnestly desire spiritual gifts, especially that you may prophesy."

The spiritual gifts, including prophecy, must be rooted in love to function as God intended. In fact, I would go so far as to say that using prophecy outside of love is manipulation—a form of witchcraft. Witchcraft isn't limited to occult practices; at its core, it involves manipulating something Godly for personal gain.

Manipulation is an easy trap to fall into, and we must remain vigilant against it as we grow in prophetic ministry. Verses 2 and 3 of First Corinthians 14 explain, "For one who speaks in a tongue does not speak to men but to God... But one who prophesies speaks to men for edification, exhortation, and consolation." These verses beautifully highlight the heart behind prophecy—it's not about the person delivering the word but about the impact on those receiving it. Prophecy exists to build up, encourage, and comfort others.

Let's unpack these three purposes:

1. **Edification:** In the original Greek, this term is tied to architecture, referring to the act of building. In a spiritual sense, it means building someone up.

2. **Exhortation:** This involves calling others closer to God through encouragement, admonition, or supplication.

3. **Consolation:** Comforting those who are in distress or need reassurance. While some translations omit "consolation," its inclusion offers a fuller picture of prophecy's purpose.

Each prophetic word should encompass all three elements: edification, exhortation, and consolation. Prophecy isn't about personal gain or status; it's about serving others and helping them grow in their relationship with God.

Verses 4 and 5 state, "One who speaks in a tongue edifies himself; but one who prophesies edifies the church..." This reiterates that prophecy benefits the community rather than exalting the individual. A common stereotype about prophetic people is that we feel an overwhelming burden to share every word we receive. However, it's crucial to discern how and when to deliver a prophetic word.

Most prophetic words God gives me are meant for private settings rather than public platforms. Many are shared in quiet, personal moments—during a conversation in a coffee shop, while meeting someone in a store aisle, speaking to a waitress, or sitting next to someone on an airplane. Sometimes, they happen in meetings with small teams or individuals. While there is a place for public, pulpit-driven prophecy, it's not the sole context for this gift.

It's also vital to remember that prophecy is never about self-promotion. Instead, it's about allowing God to speak through us to bless and uplift others. Whether delivered in public or private, prophecy's purpose is to reveal God's heart and bring His comfort, encouragement, and guidance.

By focusing on God's love, seeing people through His eyes, and maintaining humility, we can grow in prophetic ministry in a way that glorifies God and blesses the church.

- *Secret Treehouse Language*

One rarely discussed concept in prophetic circles is something I call the "secret treehouse language." Think of it as the secret code you and your childhood friends created to communicate—a language only you understood. You could speak in this code, and your friends would instantly recognize it was you.

In a similar way, we each have a unique language with God. Many books attempt to provide generalized prophetic dictionaries to help people interpret symbols in visions or messages. While these resources have been helpful to me at times, I've discovered that I'm far more accurate in hearing God's voice when I rely on our "secret language."

Let me illustrate this with a hypothetical scenario. Suppose you and I both have the same prophetic vision: we see an eagle soaring higher and higher. How would you interpret it? Many might say it symbolizes "freedom," "protection," or "gaining a better perspective." For me, however, it would signify God elevating me to a new level in the prophetic.

Who is correct? The truth is, we're all right.

Prophetic visions don't always have a universal interpretation. Each of us has a unique relationship with God, shaped by our life experiences and understanding. As long as the interpretation aligns with the Word of God, it is valid.

When I prophesy over someone, I don't merely interpret what I see or hear. I translate the "secret language" that God and I have developed over time. This personal language allows me to communicate God's message in the clearest and most relatable way for the person receiving it. The goal isn't just to interpret but to convey God's heart with clarity and simplicity.

- ***WWH Concept***

The last concept I want to expound upon is something I haven't heard much about—if at all. I've coined it the WWH concept. As the name suggests, it consists of three parts. It's not complicated, but it became profoundly impactful for me once I understood it. When delivering a prophetic word, we must ensure we know what God wants to say to the person. This requires waiting on the Lord to receive as much as possible before encountering them. For most people, this is relatively straightforward, and I'll address it in greater detail in the chapter titled "Language of Pastors." However, for *nabi* prophetic individuals like myself, we often only need an initial word or prompting to get started. Still, if we approach giving a prophetic word without knowing the specific *"what"* we're meant to communicate, we need to wait until God makes it clear.

Another challenge prophetic people frequently encounter is communicating prophetic words or encounters effectively to the intended recipient. That's why I developed a method to make the sharing process more fruitful, increasing the likelihood that the word will be received. Often, the issues arise because we deliver the word at the wrong time— perhaps in the wrong season of life for the recipient, or when they're busy, engaged in conversation, or simply not ready to receive it. We need to discern the "when" to share the prophetic word. I wait on the Holy Spirit for the go-ahead before delivering the word.

Lastly, we need to discern "how" to deliver the word. Prophetic etiquette is essential here. It's not just about delivering the message but understanding whether we're to simply speak the word, accompany it with a prophetic act, or take another approach. I don't want to offer rigid guidelines that limit how you feel led to act. God has an infinite number of ways to communicate His word, and we should explore with Him how He would like us to deliver it.

This is the heart of the "WWH" concept: knowing what, when, and how to deliver the word. Once I started applying this framework to the words God entrusted to me, I noticed far less rejection and far more receptiveness. People were ready to champion the word much more often. While this isn't a foolproof plan, it has significantly increased the likelihood of the word being received and embraced.

These insights are just a few things I've learned over the years that are rarely taught, if at all. While there are hundreds, if not thousands, of books on the prophetic, countless conferences every year, and an abundance of prophetic groups on social media, these topics often remain overlooked. Some of you might already be doing these things instinctively without realizing it. For others, this may be a freeing revelation, helping you overcome some of the roadblocks you've encountered in prophetic ministry.

CHAPTER FIVE

---••••◆•••••---

PASSION OF PURSUIT

---••••◆•••••---

O ur deepest passion should be the personal pursuit of discovering the Father's heart—not only for ourselves but for all of humanity. This journey is not optional; it is foundational and serves as the catalyst for the entire Kingdom of God. It fuels the prophetic ministry, infusing authenticity and depth into the messages we share. As we align ourselves with God's purposes, we are empowered to speak words of life, encouragement, and wisdom to others. The prophetic is not merely about special insights; it is about partnering with God's heart to bring transformation and reveal His love to the world.

In engaging with the prophetic, we must continually evaluate our motivations, ensuring our focus remains on seeking God's heart rather than pursuing gifts for their own sake. This requires a deliberate choice to prioritize a relationship with God above the desire for supernatural abilities. While the gifts of the Spirit are significant, they must remain secondary to our devotion to God. If our pursuit centers on demonstrating spiritual authority or seeking recognition rather than knowing God, we have already missed the mark.

The true prophetic flows from intimacy with God and reflects His character, which is rooted in love.

It is easy to become preoccupied with seeking spiritual gifts, as commended by Paul in 1 Corinthians 14:1: "Pursue love, yet desire earnestly spiritual gifts, especially that you may prophesy." Yet, we must first establish ourselves on the foundation of love as described in 1 Corinthians 13. The profound reminder in verse 2—"If I have the gift of prophecy, and know all mysteries and all knowledge, and if I have all faith, so as to remove mountains, but do not have love, I am nothing"—underscores the truth that without love, even the greatest gifts lose their true value.

The power of prophetic ministry does not lie in foretelling events or delivering profound words but in revealing God's heart to His people. When love is its foundation, the prophetic becomes a conduit through which God's compassion, grace, and truth are made manifest. Without love, our prophetic efforts are in vain. It is love that gives our words meaning, reflecting the very nature of God, who is love. Thus, our prophetic words should always aim to build up and strengthen the Body of Christ rather than showcase spiritual gifts.

In my earlier years of prophetic ministry, I personally fell into the trap of performing for ministry, basing my identity on the level or accuracy of the words I gave. Over time, I found myself prophesying less outside of corporate ministry opportunities, to the point where that part of my calling was nearly nonexistent. No more prophesying to people in store aisles or to waitstaff—opportunities I once embraced wholeheartedly. Instead, the prophetic ministry became an idol in my heart, overshadowing the purpose and destiny Jesus paid for, which is to bring people into the fullness of His love and plan for their lives. My focus shifted to self-gain rather than others' growth, and I've seen this same pitfall affect countless other prophetic people.

The Holy Spirit addressed this in a powerful way during a meeting at my home church. While worshiping in an amazing atmosphere of God's presence, I suddenly heard Him speak loud and clear: "That trap you keep seeing in the prophetic community—and in yourself—can be overcome. It can be consumed within the awareness of My presence and the pursuit of My heart." God revealed that when I am aware of His presence, my desires align with His. In that awareness, I live in awe of Him, with my eyes and ears fixated on Him alone.

Our primary focus must be desiring an awareness of His presence above all else. The prophetic rests outside of performance and thrives within the intimate experience of His presence. In His presence, we find growth, expansion, promotion, and deeper faith. It is here that we fully grasp God's heart, developing sensitivity to His voice and ministering from a place of mercy, humility, and compassion. Without prioritizing the pursuit of God Himself, we risk reducing the prophetic to a mere display of ability—lacking authenticity and potentially causing harm if not aligned with His purposes.

As prophetic people, we must remember that the journey is as significant as the destination. In fact, I propose that the journey is more important than the destination, as the destination has already been promised to us through Christ since the foundation of the world. The journey, however, is where the beauty lies. It is not a robotic or forced path but a dynamic ebb and flow of life. In both challenging and joyful seasons, our relationship with God deepens and flourishes.

Protecting that relationship must remain our top priority, especially as we pursue the prophetic. We are not merely chasing after gifts or experiences but seeking to dwell in the presence of the One who is the ultimate source of all good things. All spiritual gifts, while wonderful and powerful, find their true value only within the context of God's love. Without this love as the foundation, even our noblest pursuits fall short. Therefore, our foremost passion must always be to seek awareness of and abide in His presence. It is in Him that we uncover the true essence of the prophetic.

Prophetic ministry transcends personal gain or recognition, urging us to align with God's purposes for others and the world. It calls us to step into a realm where we serve as vessels of His love, ministering encouragement, comfort, and exhortation to bring healing and hope.

This alignment demands a lifestyle of surrender and pursuit—a continual seeking of God's heart not just for ourselves, but for those He places along our paths. It is an invitation to die to self and allow His love to flow through us, bringing transformation in the same way God spoke creation into being. What an honor that is—one that should leave us in constant awe and humility.

Desiring awareness of His presence leads us into deeper growth and maturity. In His presence, we learn humility, recognizing that the prophetic is not about elevating ourselves but about exalting Christ to everyone around us. We are reminded that without Him, we can do nothing. It is only through the empowerment of the Holy Spirit—the grace He extends—that we can minister effectively. This dependence keeps us grounded in God, not our gifts. In His presence, we confront our weaknesses, allowing Him to refine us and prepare us to carry His heart more fully. It is there that our faith grows, as we learn to trust Him more deeply.

Pursuing God's heart transforms our character. The more we seek awareness of His presence, the more we are conformed to His likeness. Prophetic ministry then becomes not merely an experience but a lifestyle, where we consistently reflect God's divine nature. As we abide in Him, His love, peace, and joy overflow into all areas of our lives, touching everyone we encounter. Our pursuit becomes evident not only in the words we speak but in the lives we live out before others.

The prophetic life calls us to embody the message of God's love and restoration, reaching out to the broken and bringing hope to the hopeless. The lifestyle of a prophetic person is one where the words we speak are weightier than mere sound; they become a tangible reflection of God's heart. Through this, people—often for the first time—experience what it is like to be truly seen by God.

Ultimately, the journey of discovering the Father's heart continually draws us deeper, inviting us to lay aside distractions and prioritize our relationship with God above all else. This focus is crucial to remaining grounded and faithful to the call upon our lives. When grounded in the pursuit of God's love and presence, the prophetic becomes a powerful tool for bringing life, encouragement, and transformation. It ceases to be about us and becomes a conduit through which God reveals Himself to the world.

Let us be stirred to seek Him first, love Him deeply, and allow that love to shape every aspect of our lives, especially in the prophetic. When the foundation is right, the gifts will follow naturally and find their proper place. In pursuing the Father's heart, we discover the true meaning and power of the prophetic—not as an end in itself, but as a means to reveal God's love and bring His kingdom to earth.

CHAPTER SIX

―――――――― ·····•••‹❧›•••····· ――――――――

WHAT THE HECK IS A PROPHET
ANYWAYS?

―――――――― ·····•••‹❧›•••····· ――――――――

F inally, let's dive in. I've had the privilege of preaching across various denominations, from churches where speaking in tongues and spiritual gifts were seen as essential to every gathering, to others that believed such manifestations ceased with the Apostles. This range of experiences has given me a broad view of the diverse landscape within the body of Christ. I grew up in a Presbyterian church but later pastored a congregation immersed in revival culture.

My upbringing was steeped in ministry; two of my uncles were pastors, and my grandmother's life revolved around the church. In our blended family, my biological father was absent, and my mother and stepfather raised me and my two younger brothers, as well as my two brothers from my stepfather's side. We began attending a local Presbyterian church when I was old enough for confirmation—a class where young people profess their faith and learn the fundamentals of Christianity. The church was situated in a small town of fewer than 50 people, typical of northwest

Iowa, where most towns had populations under 500. Despite this, the church's youth group drew over 50 kids each week from several surrounding towns, creating a vibrant community.

Then, something happened that I didn't fully understand at the time. One Sunday, during a regular sermon, a respected elder spoke in tongues, and another elder interpreted. This event stunned the congregation, as such manifestations were viewed as relics of the past, not relevant for today. Shortly afterward, the pastor was dismissed, and the church's membership dwindled. My family left the church—not because we opposed tongues—my mother actually believed in it, having been baptized in the Holy Spirit as a teenager—but because our family's lives were heading in a different direction outside of the faith.

Nearly a decade later, after living a life far removed from the church, I had a transformative encounter with God in the basement of my house in Elkhorn, Nebraska. I was in the lowest place of my life, and God's love overwhelmed me in a way I'd never known. Up until that encounter, I had been arrogant, selfish, and dismissive of others, hiding my pain behind a façade. I had faced internal battles since childhood, experiencing demonic oppression and struggling with self-worth. My identity was tied to my performance in various pursuits, yet I could never seem to gain real momentum in life. I would look for opportunities to prove to everyone that I was something that I really wasn't.

Everything changed when I read Spirit Wars by Kris Vallotton. It was as if God had embedded the answer I'd been searching for in the pages of that book: the realization that the enemy hated what I was created for. The internal battles I faced were attempts to keep me from my divine calling. As I continued in ministry, I made many mistakes—seeking acceptance, trying to imitate other ministers, and succumbing to old lies I believed in my childhood. I learned these missteps were rooted in not having found my "tribe"—people who truly understood and resonated with my journey.

Years later, another book by Vallotton, Destined to Win, gave me further clarity. I realized that while the mentors, ministry relationships, and friends I'd had were good people and were good to me, they weren't necessarily my tribe. There were mismatched expectations—some unspoken and others unmet. Although these individuals were remarkable, they didn't belong in my inner circle, which needed to be filled with those who could walk with me in my God-given purpose and also me with them.

I felt it was necessary to share a brief history leading up to this revelation, even though there's so much more I could have included about God's amazing works in my life. It truly has been a journey from the rags of the world to the riches of the Kingdom of God. Every struggle, setback, flaw, and challenge I've faced prepared me to be the husband and father I am today—something that wasn't exemplified in the lives of those I grew up around. It's a profound honor to fulfill these roles, which I've long desired, and I'm incredibly blessed to have them. I would sacrifice ministry and spiritual gifts in a heartbeat for the sake of my wife, Roberta, and my children. They come after my pursuit of God but before everything else.

This wasn't always the case. There was a time when my ministry consumed me, despite my efforts to avoid that. I thought I had achieved some form of balance, and my wife graciously supported me while I struggled to understand why it felt as though my identity was tied to running at full speed in prophetic ministry. When I wasn't doing that, I felt off—almost unclean, as if I wasn't truly myself. If others didn't allow the prophetic to flow, I took it as a personal attack on who I was.

Then, I experienced a pivotal moment of revelation in another encounter with God. I realized that God created me with a specific purpose, and that Christ didn't just give five gifts or graces to the church, as I'd previously understood from Ephesians 4. Instead, He gave five distinct types of people—apostles, prophets, evangelists, pastors, and teachers—as tools to serve the church and equip the body of Christ toward full maturity in Him. This understanding shifted my perspective, transforming how I approached both ministry and life.

Hear my heart on this—I almost cringe as I write it. I truly dislike titles and being labeled, but I feel the need to address this for the sake of clarity and understanding. I've encountered many people who believe they are apostles, prophets, or hold some other five-fold ministry office, often because of the cultural influence within their spiritual environment. I understand—it's normal in certain settings. But there are also false representations, and we need to be cautious about assigning titles to ourselves or imposing expectations on others that don't align with what God has truly called them to be.

What I've come to understand deeply is that God knew me before I was even in my mother's womb. He created me with a purpose—to be a prophet on this earth. My calling is to equip the saints to hear God's voice for themselves, to build them up, and to call forth the destiny that God has planted within each of His children I encounter. It's about nurturing that God-given potential and bringing it into fullness.

I can almost hear the questions you're asking: How do you know for sure you are? How do I know if I am? What makes you a prophet? What makes me a prophet? What makes (insert your favorite prophet's name) a prophet?

To answer these questions honestly, we must turn to the scriptures. Over and over again, we see similar situations occur in the lives of the prophets in the Bible. These patterns give us insight into what often defines a prophetic calling.

Most prophets in the Bible had clear, documented encounters with God before they were officially called or recognized as prophets. Consider these examples:

1. **Moses:** Moses encountered God in the burning bush before being called to lead Israel out of Egypt (Exodus 3:1-10). This pivotal moment defined his mission.

2. **Samuel:** As a child, Samuel heard God calling him while serving under Eli in the temple. This occurred before he became a renowned prophet (1 Samuel 3:1-10).

3. **Isaiah:** Isaiah had a dramatic vision of the Lord seated on His throne, surrounded by seraphim, before he received his prophetic commission. He responded with the iconic words, "Here am I; send me" (Isaiah 6:1-8).

4. **Jeremiah:** God spoke directly to Jeremiah, declaring, "Before I formed you in the womb I knew you, and before you were born I consecrated you; I have appointed you a prophet to the nations" (Jeremiah 1:5).

Despite feeling unqualified due to his youth, Jeremiah eventually accepted the call (Jeremiah 1:4-10).

5. **Ezekiel:** Ezekiel experienced a powerful vision of God's glory by the river Chebar, involving living creatures, wheels, and the likeness of a throne. This encounter marked the start of his prophetic ministry (Ezekiel 1).

6. **Amos:** Amos was a herdsman and gatherer of sycamore fruit when God called him to prophesy. He later described how God took him from following the flock and commanded him to speak to Israel (Amos 7:14-15).

7. **Elisha:** Although Elisha's calling came through the prophet Elijah, it was God's authority that ordained him. Elijah symbolically cast his mantle on Elisha while he was plowing in the field, initiating his prophetic journey (1 Kings 19:19-21).

8. **Jonah:** Jonah received a direct command from God to go and prophesy against Nineveh. His initial reluctance led to the well-known episode with the great fish (Jonah 1:1-3).

9. **Hosea:** God spoke directly to Hosea, instructing him to marry an unfaithful wife as a symbolic representation

of Israel's spiritual infidelity. This marked the beginning of Hosea's ministry (Hosea 1:2).

These examples show how God often initiated contact with future prophets, preparing and commissioning them for their roles. While the nature of these encounters varied, each served to affirm the prophet's calling and establish their ministry.

These encounters are deeply personal and life-changing, but they don't entirely define who is or isn't a prophet. They are just the beginning. The next critical element is the recognition of the calling by mature followers of Jesus and leaders in the body of Christ who act with wisdom and integrity. A genuine prophetic calling will be evident, and the affirmation of others is crucial. However, this part of the process is often the most challenging and painful.

You might have had a profound encounter with God and feel the weight of your calling. It's like holding a secret you're desperate to share, but you must wait to be tested and proven. This is where many stumble, rushing ahead of God's timing.

I've seen it happen in many ways. Some hastily establish platforms—building websites, going live on social media, starting YouTube channels, or seeking speaking engagements to proclaim their calling. Others confront their pastors or church leaders, demanding recognition or a position. Some, frustrated by a lack of affirmation, leave the church entirely to pursue their ministry independently. And then there are those who retreat, metaphorically hiding in caves, allowing the calling to go unfulfilled.

We'll address these common flaws in later chapters, diving into how to prepare, become self-aware, and overcome the stereotypes that prophetic people often face. The aim is to pinpoint these characteristic weaknesses and counter them with strategies that allow us to sharpen our calling and, more importantly, gain the acceptance we need to fulfill our purpose effectively.

So, what should we do? The answer lies less in announcing our calling and more in the posture of our hearts. We must never forget that the purpose of the five-fold ministry—and especially the role of the prophet—is to serve the body of Christ. We are instruments designed to build up the church, not to seek honor for ourselves, but to honor others; not to gain recognition, but to pour out what has been entrusted to us. This mindset can be especially challenging for those of us who have faced rejection. I know I'm jumping ahead here, but rejection is an all-too-familiar theme for prophetic people. Our words and visions are often dismissed, not because they lack substance, but because we sometimes struggle to communicate them effectively.

Prophetic individuals often find it difficult to express what they receive from the Holy Spirit. These revelations are vivid—sometimes more vivid than anything else—and we can become so consumed with passion that our delivery overshadows the message itself, leading to misunderstandings.

Now, let's get practical.

What's the next step? Serve. Serve humbly and, if possible, serve quietly. Be present. Stay alert to the "Cracks" (and yes, we'll explore this more in the Cracks Chapter), as recognizing these moments will help you steward prophetic words wisely in the current season. When you feel led to share something, bring it to the leadership and then step back. Hand it over. Let them decide how to act on it; that responsibility is not yours to bear.

This approach serves several key purposes:

1. It reveals your character when you offer your gift freely, without expectation.

2. It allows you to share the responsibility for prophetic words as you grow, rather than carrying their full weight alone.

3. It demonstrates your willingness to submit your gift to mature leadership, which builds trust.

4. Most importantly, it provides an opportunity for leaders to affirm the calling on your life.

It's equally crucial to be discerning about where you seek guidance and how you engage with others. Connecting with a prophetic community or other prophets is essential for growth. Ideally, this would be within your home church. If that's not possible, look for such a community elsewhere in your city or online. But be intentional about choosing a group that is spiritually healthy, mature, and trustworthy. The guidance and support you receive will profoundly influence your development and effectiveness in your calling.

It's worth noting that seeking a prophetic community doesn't mean abandoning your church if one doesn't exist there. It means supplementing your spiritual growth while remaining committed to your home church. This balance is important for staying rooted and accountable while still receiving the support you need.

~~~~~~~~

A side note:

You might be the one God is calling to establish a prophetic community in your local church. If so, embrace that role with courage. Pioneering isn't easy, but it creates a space where others can grow and flourish in their prophetic gifts, just as you are growing in yours.

CHAPTER SEVEN

CRACKS

I think this is one of the most pivotal lessons I've learned as a filter for the calling of the prophet and the prophetic. Once we move past the urge to share everything that comes to us and begin applying the WWH concept we discussed in Chapter 4, there's one last, and in my belief, most crucial understanding we need to grasp as we step forward in our prophetic gifting.

Let me tell you the story of how I came to understand the concept of cracks. It was during one of the most challenging seasons of my ministry. I was on staff at a church where we uncovered significant corruption—financial mismanagement and other issues that impacted both leadership and the congregation. Leaders from the network our church was part of had noticed from afar that something wasn't right. Deciding to investigate further, they boarded a plane without warning and arrived in our city.

The first meeting took place on Good Friday. One of the leaders sat in the front row, observing, and quickly realized that the situation warranted deeper questioning. Over the following three weeks, events unraveled—there were intense meetings and probing conversations. Ultimately, the network concluded that it would be best for me to transition out of the church. They encouraged me to pursue my calling while they worked to guide the church back on course and address the senior pastor's missteps. Their hope was to help the pastor find restoration while also regaining control of the church. However, the senior pastor chose a different path, ignoring the network's guidance. Within months, the church closed abruptly, surrounded by controversy.

I share this to emphasize a hard truth I learned during those weeks: many of the issues could have been avoided—or at least mitigated—if I had understood the concept of cracks and discerned how to navigate them. During that intense three-week period, one of the leaders called and invited my wife and me to dinner at a local steakhouse. Now, I can't resist a good steak, and I greatly respected this man of God, so of course, we accepted.

At the restaurant, as we sat down with him and his wife—a sweet, quiet woman who rarely spoke—something unexpected happened. She looked me directly in the eye and said, "Andrew, I want to hear the truth. Not the polished version where you try to honor people by holding back. Tell us everything—what has happened and what is happening." I was stunned. I glanced at her husband and asked a question that had been swirling in my mind for a long time. "Why is it always me? Why am I the one who has to expose these things? Can't I just be a normal guy working at a church?"

His expression turned serious, filled with both compassion and gravity. He replied, "No, you can't, because you're not just a normal guy. You're like me. I've had to expose many situations over the years. It's not easy, but it's what God has called us to do."

That answer hit me like a freight train, but it wasn't the end of the conversation. My next question came out so fast I barely had time to think. "Okay, but how do you know which things you're supposed to expose and which ones you're supposed to serve and fix?"

His reply felt like a ton of bricks: "They're like cracks. Some cracks aren't structural—they don't need fixing or exposing. God will address those in His time, as part of the journey. Then there are cracks He shows you so you can fix them—through prayer, relationship, or service. These cracks are repaired quietly, without anyone knowing. Finally, there are structural cracks. These are the ones you have to put a wedge into and hammer open because they need to be exposed to the light. These cracks affect the entire structure and the well-being of the people within it. The Spirit will show you which is which."

That lesson at Firehouse Grill changed everything for me. I started reevaluating past words I had given through the lens of cracks, and it stung. I saw how many times I had missed the mark, assuming everything needed to be said and heard. From that moment on, everything had to pass through this filter.

At first, seeing through the lens of cracks unintentionally led me into another pattern—I began judging people based solely on the flaws I perceived in them. I would focus entirely on their cracks instead of viewing them as God sees them. It took me time to understand that the cracks weren't the essence of who they were. Instead, the cracks were the false beliefs or areas of brokenness they were living out.

For a long time, this distorted my perspective, making it difficult for me to see the whole person beneath the flaws I noticed. But as I returned to seeking God's heart, I began asking Him why He loved these people, even with their cracks. In that process, I discovered something profound: God's love for them was unwavering, no matter what I saw.

It was then that I began to separate what I was observing— the cracks—from the truth of who God said they were. With this understanding, I could approach each person with both compassion and clarity. I could discern more clearly what, if anything, needed to be addressed about their "crack," but always within the context of their identity as

God created and sees them. This allowed me to respond to people with grace rather than judgment, viewing their cracks not as defining them but as areas needing healing or transformation.

Let's examine each type of crack, as situations are rarely black and white. As we grow in understanding, we may discover that a single crack has multiple fractures, or several smaller cracks that have the potential to grow into larger issues. The possibilities are endless when dealing with these cracks, but we must always be led by the Spirit of God.

The most common type of crack is the small fracture. Often, these cracks don't need to be openly exposed but can be healed through prayer, building relationships, or acts of service. You might be wondering, "How can this be addressed through service or relationships?" The answer is simple: people need unconditional love, free from expectations or personal gain. Many times, God has revealed fractured areas in others, and rather than confronting or distancing myself from them, I chose to love, encourage, and serve them. I offered words of prophetic edification and stood as their strongest advocate. What others may see as character flaws are often survival mechanisms developed because of a lack of genuine, unconditional love in their lives. Love drives out fear (1 John 4:18), and love covers a multitude of sins (1 Peter 4:8).

It's crucial to be aware of our gifts and the common weaknesses within our prophetic community, as situations are rarely clear-cut. We must stay committed to people and ministries far beyond the point where we prophetic people and communities tend to make an early exit. I've personally severed ties too soon in the past, influenced by seeing everything through a rigid, black-and-white lens. Yet, within the prophetic gift and calling, it's said of John the Baptist, with the spirit of Elijah, that he came "to turn the hearts of the fathers to the children, and the disobedient to the wisdom of the just, to make ready a people prepared for the Lord" (Luke 1:17). We are called to the ministry of Jesus, which is fundamentally a ministry of reconciliation. Our purpose is to turn hearts back to Jesus and toward one another, bringing reconciliation to all of humanity and unity with God.

The next crack we need to examine is what I call the hidden crack. Whether the person is hiding it out of shame or they are simply unaware of it, it's still a bigger issue than the small fracture, though not necessarily urgent or catastrophic. The impact of this crack isn't yet critical to the person or those around them, but it's still important.

Hidden cracks should be addressed privately, as the saying goes, "behind closed doors." This doesn't mean keeping them secret but acknowledging that they don't require public confrontation. These matters are best handled with discretion and care, focusing on restoration rather than exposure. These situations require a personal, one-on-one approach or small group intervention, emphasizing the importance of strong relationships. If the Holy Spirit reveals a hidden crack but you lack a personal connection with the individual or ministry, the best course of action is to entrust the matter to leadership or someone experienced in addressing such issues with love and mercy. Relationship is key in handling these situations with wisdom and care.

When addressing hidden cracks, we must approach with a gentle heart rooted in reconciliation, but also firm in truth. It's important to enter these conversations with humility, especially since prophetic people tend to see things in black and white. Recognizing this tendency, we must come "low," approaching the person or ministry with no agenda other than a genuine desire to help repair the crack. We should be willing to give everything while expecting nothing in return, including the possibility of being rejected or denied the opportunity to address the issue.

Not everyone will want their cracks fixed or may even deny that a crack exists. We must be prepared for our insights to go unreceived. If we approach with a mindset of gaining something, we are bound to take offense if rejected. However, if we come solely with the intention to love, there is no opportunity for offense to take root in our hearts.

More often than not, when we address a crack with a person or ministry, it's well-received because we approach it with humility and communicate it gently. However, that wasn't always the case. In the past, I would come in aggressively, pointing out the crack, emphasizing its severity, and backing it up with scripture, expecting immediate change or ready to drive a wedge in and crack the situation wide open. As you might expect, this rarely worked. I have since transitioned away from this approach after receiving the revelation of the cracks. However, this remains a challenging area for prophetic people and prophets.

Over the years, many young prophetic people have come to me, seeking wisdom or grappling with questions about interpreting dreams, visions, or navigating life as a prophetic person. One recurring theme I've noticed is that many prophetic individuals struggle with seeing cracks— they perceive dirt, sin, and flaws, but they aren't sure how to handle them. Often, the default response is to unload everything they see or hear, but that isn't the most effective approach. When we're just beginning in our prophetic walk, this may be all we know, but it's not the best way. While this could be a chapter of its own, let me briefly touch on it.

I call this concept "upside-down prophecy." Prophetic people often see sin, darkness, or flaws in someone or something, but we're rarely taught how to communicate those insights constructively. Over time, I learned the power of our prophetic words and adopted a reversed approach. For example, if I sense someone is struggling with addiction to pornography while praying for them, instead of pointing out the sin of lust, I would prophesy the opposite: "I see the Lord taking you into a season of increased purity, calling you to live a holy, pure life." Instead of empowering the problem, I'm speaking life into the solution with my words. This approach—focusing on calling people into their God-given potential—shifts the atmosphere and allows space for true transformation through the Holy Spirit.

I learned this lesson the hard way. There's a story I'd like to share that might expose me a bit, but it's important for context. A good friend of mine, eager to find a wife, had been going on dates with Christian women but couldn't find the right connection. Casually, I mentioned a single woman from another church who was in a similar situation, suggesting he could consider her "if all else fails." I knew both parties were in different places in their lives, and the comment was flippant and not rooted in wisdom. A few weeks later, my friend excitedly told me he had met someone he felt deeply connected with and showed me her picture on Instagram. To my shock, it was the same woman I had casually mentioned.

At that moment, I had to backtrack and own my mistake. I apologized, explained why my initial comment was unwise, and shared the full context. My friend continued to date her, but eventually, they realized they weren't a good fit for each other. That situation taught me a valuable lesson: my words have the power to create avenues for things to happen. I realized I could have saved him heartache, time, and trust by being more cautious with my words.

As I sought the Lord for insight into my mistake, He led me to 2 Kings 2, where Elisha cursed a group of boys who mocked him, and two bears came out and attacked and killed them. God showed me that I needed to be careful with my words, reminding me that He created me to speak life and that I hold the authority to create both right and wrong things with my words. That conviction was so strong that I got a tattoo of a bear's head on my knee as a personal reminder of this lesson.

This understanding has been crucial for me, especially when addressing hidden cracks. When confronting difficult or uncomfortable situations, I now recognize my authority to speak life into fractured areas. If God grants me the opportunity to help repair a crack, I need the wisdom to communicate the necessary steps for restoration. In these cases, I often use the "upside-down prophecy" tactic, knowing that most of us aren't yet living in the fullness of what God has called us to. If we were all in perfect alignment, God wouldn't need to call us forward—He calls us because there's still growth to pursue.

Now, let's examine the last type of crack: Structural Cracks. These are the cracks that not only affect the individual but also play a significant role in the foundational structure of something larger, impacting or potentially influencing a group of people. Sometimes, this crack is holding up a larger structure that is influencing many people.

These cracks need to be handled with surgical precision. We must approach leadership, the board, or those with influence over the individual or ministry, and communicate clearly, humbly, and firmly. Like the hidden crack, Structural Cracks require care, but they usually necessitate firmer communication, grounded in truth and the leading of the Holy Spirit. It's essential that prophetic people are mature and ready before attempting to tackle such cracks, and it's even better not to handle them alone.

Let me explain. I was pastoring at the time, driving with a couple of fellow pastors to a leadership conference. As we were enjoying the ride down I-80 west of Omaha, God began speaking to me about another ministry in our city—a new church that was growing rapidly and capturing the entire city's attention. Not only was this church growing fast, but it was also utilizing social media in innovative ways. Many churches in our city were still behind when it came to adopting technology, but this church was effectively leveraging it to expand its reach. Since then, every church in our city has significantly increased its online presence, helping spread God's love far and wide.

I had been praying for this church and its pastor for a few months, and that day, as I sat in the backseat of the truck, God revealed some troubling things about the pastor and the ministry. I shared these revelations with the two ministers with me. One of them knew the leadership that had sent this pastor out to plant the church, so we decided to call them while on the road. I shared what God had shown me, but in hindsight, I realize I didn't communicate it in the best way. It wasn't the worst, but it certainly wasn't my best. The leadership dismissed my word, confidently stating that such things weren't happening and that I was mistaken. I apologized, and we moved on.

A little over a year later, everything God had shown me came to pass. The pastor was removed from his position, and both his family and the church were left in turmoil. Thankfully, the church leadership handled the situation as best as they could, and the church is now thriving under a new pastor with the highest integrity. When the announcement was made, a friend of mine FaceTimed me right in the middle of it, and it felt like a bomb had gone off in that room. People were weeping, confused, and deeply hurt. When I got off the phone, I was completely undone. God had shown me this more than a year before it happened, and if the leadership had received the word I gave, they might have been able to intervene, help the pastor, and potentially prevent this disaster.

At first, I felt angry that they hadn't received the warning, but then God, in His way, met me and showed me that this was a learning experience—a lesson in how to communicate challenging revelations. I'm a passionate person, especially when it comes to words from God, but sometimes my passion can be misinterpreted. God revealed that while passion is good, the way I communicated needed to change. I had been shown things at critical moments when a sinking ship could be righted, but my approach often made it difficult for others to receive the message. The accuracy of the word was there, but the delivery was lacking.

This experience taught me the importance of communicating even the hardest revelations in a way that opens doors for redemption. The "upside-down prophecy" concept is crucial here as well. In these situations, I've learned to share what I saw but also emphasize that God has a redemptive plan for every situation. I now pair my insights with biblical promises of God's desire for restoration. This approach not only acknowledges the reality of the problem but also calls forth hope and invites others to partner with God in His redemptive work.

It's one thing to see the cracks; it's another thing to confront them. But if we confront the cracks in the wrong way, we'll never be able to partner with the ministry of Christ, which is reconciliation. We must keep this responsibility in the forefront of our minds when dealing with cracks.

CHAPTER EIGHT

THE LIGHT SWITCH

In my early years of prophetic ministry, I often felt overwhelmed by the sheer intensity of the gift, as though divine insight were flowing through me like a firehose, surging through my thoughts and words. It was as if I were carrying a weight so immense that surrendering to it seemed the only way to find any relief. While this intensity wasn't unwelcome, its heaviness was undeniable, making it difficult to connect with others—especially those who hadn't experienced such profound spiritual encounters. Relating to "ordinary people" seemed impossible; I knew they couldn't fully comprehend the unique, often surreal world I was navigating.

Nights became vivid landscapes of intense dreams, often accompanied by battles with demonic opposition. Each morning, I had to reconcile these otherworldly experiences with the practical demands of both work and ministry. Transitioning from a secular job to full-time ministry stirred an internal storm, despite the outward success that was visible in the ministry itself. Often, I found myself in my office at the church I was pastoring, lost in visions, only to awaken on the floor, enveloped in the deep presence of

God. Crowds in public became a source of anxiety, with prophetic words rising so quickly they drowned out everything else, overwhelming me. These encounters brought peace and insight to others, revealing hidden truths and aligning them with God's purpose. But the cost was steep: sleepless nights and intense spiritual warfare. At times, I feared that if people knew the full extent of my experiences, they might question my grasp on reality.

Then, during an e-course called Emerging Prophets by Keith Ferrante, I heard a simple yet transformative statement: "The gift is like a light switch. You can turn it off when you need a break or want to be present with your family." At first, I was stunned. Then, anger rose within me—why had I endured so much without knowing this was possible? Ferrante's words clashed with my understanding of "God the relentless pursuer," but they revealed a crucial truth: God doesn't impose Himself on us or manipulate us spiritually. This revelation reframed how I carried the gift, marking one of the most liberating lessons I've encountered.

However, it wasn't an easy journey. I wrestled with a fundamental question: Could I really have the authority to ask for a break? Could I simply say, "Not right now"? I needed biblical grounding and a deeper understanding. First, as prophetic people, we are children of God above all else. While prophecy is the avenue through which we serve, it doesn't define our entire identity. I'm not advocating detaching from our calling, but rather recognizing the freedom God gives us to choose balance. This message is directed specifically to prophets, not merely to those with prophetic gifts. Prophets are individuals chosen by God even before they were formed in their mothers' wombs, set apart to serve as a gift to the body of Christ, equipping and strengthening it. While being a prophet is an inseparable part of your identity—distinct from simply having the gift of prophecy—it doesn't mean you're bound to minister at all times. Taking moments to step back and recharge is completely within your reach. For instance, you have the right to be fully present with your family during dinner, without feeling the constant pull to minister to others.

Riding the wave of encounter after encounter can lead us to neglect those around us and the responsibilities that demand our attention. Prophetic people are also spouses, parents, friends, children, employees, etc. We must remain fully present in these roles, which requires space and time to process and reflect through the lens of Scripture.

Shortly after this revelation, I went out to dinner with my wife. Midway through the meal, God began speaking to me about our waiter. I shared these insights with him, and the young man was deeply moved, astonished by the idea that God knew him so intimately. But when I turned back to my wife, I found her looking hurt. This had become a pattern during our outings—I'd find myself ministering to strangers instead of focusing on her. Confused, I asked what was wrong, and she answered, "Sometimes I wish you'd give me the same attention you give others."

That hit me hard. Here I was, eager to encourage others, yet unintentionally sidelining my wife. Suddenly, I felt trapped in a dilemma: if I didn't prophesy, I felt guilty, but if I did, I risked hurting her. Then, in a moment of clarity, I heard God say, "She is right."

In the weeks that followed, this tension kept resurfacing. I had built my identity around ministry, believing my value was tied to actively operating in the prophetic. But I had missed a key insight: prophecy is a gift to serve others, not a measure of my worth. God's love defines me—not the function of my gift. This breakthrough helped me realign with my calling, recognizing that the prophetic wasn't the center of my identity, but rather a tool for service.

Over the years, I had struggled with feeling valued only for what I could produce—whether in sports, work, or relationships. This need for validation had, at times, led me to define my worth by what I could give or do. But then I grasped a liberating truth: my value isn't measured by my usefulness. If God can use a donkey to speak, then being used by Him doesn't make me inherently special; it's His love and grace that shape my true identity. Made in His image, I am valued for more than my role (Matthew 6:24–

31). This understanding reoriented my life, anchoring me in God's call for me beyond any specific function.

In this spirit, I started a daily ritual to remind myself of who I am in Christ. Each morning, before getting out of bed, I ask the Holy Spirit one question: "What do You think of me today?" Then I wait. At first, this practice felt challenging—sometimes I'd sit in silence for 10 minutes, other times nearly an hour. But staying disciplined helped me move past my own feelings or thoughts about myself and instead hear directly from God. His simple affirmations, like "I'm proud of you, son," would fill me with purpose, setting the tone for my day. Sometimes, He'd share something profound; other times just a single encouraging word. But each exchange grounded my identity in His perspective.

This daily practice must be guided and refined by two key principles. First, we must always filter what we hear through Scripture, as the enemy will attempt to undermine this area. Second, what God speaks is meant to build us up, though at times His words may lovingly challenge us to grow. The voice of God brings life, never condemnation (1 Corinthians 14).

And so, I return to the central lesson: while we have this gift, we are also called to be fully present for our family, friends, and loved ones. Balance is essential. We must recognize that we, not God, sometimes impose an unending demand on ourselves. God's voice is always available to us; creation itself bears the echoes of His Word. Jesus set this example: though fully engaged in ministry, He also prioritized rest and intimate moments with His disciples and His Father in heaven.

Self-control, a portion of the fruit of the Spirit, is more than resisting a donut or holding back frustration—it's knowing when to pause, when to be present, and when to rest in the assurance of His love.

I encourage and challenge you today, as prophets and prophetic people, to take time to rest, to be present with your loved ones, your job, or even with God Himself, letting Him edify you personally.

CHAPTER NINE

--------••••◆◆••••--------

SEEING WITH YOUR EARS

--------••••◆◆••••--------

One of the most life-changing, intimate encounters I've ever had in God's presence occurred when someone I deeply respected—before we'd even truly connected—pulled me onto a stage and publicly prophesied over me, declaring me a prophet in front of 800 peers and people from the very city God had called me to. Just an hour earlier, in front of that same crowd, a highly influential pastor in our city, with whom I'd once served, embraced me, kissed me on the cheek, and reconciled with me over past grievances and mishandling. God completely overwhelmed me in that meeting—I was crying uncontrollably, a complete mess, but in the best possible way.

The same man who prophesied over me then invited me to follow him as he prayed for others after his message, asking me to prophesy with him over the people gathered. We prayed together until around 1 a.m., and the most incredible part was that it all took place in the very church where I had once served—the same place where the pastor had apologized for his past treatment of me. I had never imagined I'd be ministering in that church again, let alone be publicly affirmed as a prophet within those walls. My mind was absolutely blown.

The words from that prophecy echoed relentlessly in my mind: "You will see clearly with your ears and hear clearly through your eyes." I couldn't shake them. What did it mean? Had he mixed up the words?

It took years to grasp its significance. I sought wisdom from prophetic voices across the United States, questioning them whenever we crossed paths at churches or conferences. I poured over the Scriptures, searching for clarity, digging tirelessly. Then, one day, while reading through the Gospel of John, something extraordinary happened. As I read chapter 5, a wave of revelation washed over me. It changed everything.

Let me set the stage. In John 5, Jesus had just healed the man at the pool of Bethesda. This act enraged the Jewish leaders, who were appalled by His disregard for their long-held traditions. To them, it felt like Jesus was trampling on their sacred laws and undermining their identity.

Then came the moment that stunned everyone: in verse 17, Jesus said, "My Father is working until now, and I Myself am working." With these words, He declared equality with the Father. The shock must have left them speechless, their minds reeling.

In verse 19, Jesus elaborated: "Truly, truly, I say to you, the Son can do nothing of Himself, unless it is something He sees the Father doing; for whatever the Father does, these things the Son also does in like manner." Time seemed to stand still as I read those words. Memories of all the times I'd seen Jesus retreat to pray alone flooded back. Suddenly, it all clicked. Jesus' intimacy with the Father was so profound, so seamless, that their actions were indistinguishable. Whatever the Father did, Jesus mirrored perfectly.

This realization hit me personally. It reminded me of my son Ryder, who emulates me in uncanny ways. Though he looks like my wife, his personality, mannerisms, and even his spiritual sensitivity reflect me. It's like looking in a mirror with his personality. Ryder prays the way I pray, speaks the way I speak, disciplines the dogs the way I do—it's almost eerie. He embodies the essence of a "knighted, mounted warrior," living up to the prophetic weight of his name. Watching him is like seeing a living example of what Jesus defined Himself as—the "perfect image of the invisible God" in heaven.

This emulation that Jesus did with the Father mirrors what Ryder does with me—but on a divine level. Colossians 1:15 calls Jesus the "image of the invisible God," and in the Gospels, Jesus tells the disciples, "If you've seen Me, you've seen the Father." How? Because Jesus only did what He saw His Father doing and spoke only what He heard the Father saying. John 12:50 confirms this: "What I say, therefore, I say just as the Father has told Me."

This revelation reshaped my understanding of how Jesus operated. Every word, every action flowed from a place of profound observation and listening. Jesus went away to pray—not to speak endlessly or plead, but to align with the Father's will, to glimpse heaven's activity, and to hear His Father's voice. He listened and observed more than He spoke. That revelation floored me.

It's a level of intimacy and obedience that compels transformation. I realized that I, too, must live this way— listening, observing, and aligning every action and word with the Father's voice and movements.

We often get caught up in the concept of prayer, especially when we lean heavily on the verse, "Ask, and it will be given to you; seek, and you will find; knock, and it will be opened to you." Praise God for a Father who invites us to boldly enter His throne room and ask for His help when we need it. There are absolutely times when this kind of prayer is necessary. But more and more, I find that my prayer life has shifted. These days, I come into prayer not to present requests, but to observe, listen, and hear His voice.

Don't get me wrong—I deeply value the practice of praying in tongues and believe it's an incredible gift for all believers. But what I'm talking about here is something altogether different.

There's a remarkable story about the prophet Bob Jones that captures the heart of this shift in focus. Let me recount it, though I'm paraphrasing, and some details may not be exact—the essence of the story, however, is spot on.

An angel appeared to Bob and told him that Jesus would visit him and answer any questions he wanted to ask. Bob, naturally, was instructed to prepare. When the day came, Bob waited expectantly, but Jesus didn't appear. Confused and frustrated, he wondered what had gone wrong.

A few months later, the same angel returned with the same message: Jesus would visit him, and he should have his questions ready. Once again, Bob prepared, and once again, Jesus didn't come. This time, Bob was even more frustrated.

When the angel came a third time, he spoke with a sternness, instructing Bob to take this seriously and be ready. Though frustrated, Bob prepared himself as before. Finally, on the appointed day, Jesus appeared and asked, "What questions would you like Me to answer today, Bob?"

But instead of presenting his list of questions, Bob replied, "I have no questions to ask. I am simply willing to listen to whatever You want to tell me."

Jesus agreed, affirming that Bob's response was proper. In that moment, Jesus delivered one of the most profound prophetic words for the Body of Christ—a word so significant that its impact continues to resonate today, even beyond the charismatic and prophetic streams of the Church.

This story reshaped how I approach prayer. It reminds me that the highest posture in God's presence isn't that of a seeker with demands, but of a child who seeks their Father with open ears and an open heart.

I have become more present with God, as well as more effective in my ministry. My ears and eyes are turned to Him at all times. In the craziness of being a husband, father, business owner, and friend, it has become easier to hear His voice in all things—rather than only when I'm in the prayer closet presenting my requests.

Looking back, I wish this season of seeking had been shorter, but I see now that the journey was necessary. It cracked my heart wide open to a deeper understanding of the Holy Spirit—one that continues to shape me every day. I truly pray this increases your intimacy with the presence of God in your life.

CHAPTER TEN

MEEKNESS

Meekness: The Key to Fully Embracing Righteousness and
Our Identity in Christ

In a world that often equates power with dominance and authority with control, meekness can seem contradictory. Yet, the profound wisdom in the words, "Blessed are the meek, for they shall inherit the earth" (Matthew 5:5), invites us to reevaluate. This passage from the Beatitudes urges a deeper exploration of meekness and its connection to true dominion. To embody meekness, we must first understand the authority God has granted us. Only then can we live out meekness in its fullness.

- ***The Nature of Meekness***

Meekness is not weakness. It is the strength to surrender our authority to God, allowing Him to direct our lives according to His will. This act of yielding transforms us, giving us real power—not through dominating others, but by submitting to divine guidance. To be meek is to possess the authority to enforce power, yet choose to act with mercy and compassion, fully aligned with God's heart.

Picture a sword always by your side; meekness is choosing to keep it sheathed, even when provoked. This restraint reflects a heart that understands the mercy and grace God has extended to us time and again. Rather than using power to dominate, we choose mercy, grace, and humility. "Let your gentleness be evident to all. The Lord is near" (Philippians 4:5). This is not passivity but a deliberate exercise of authority, rooted in love.

Consider Jesus' response to Peter when he struck the guard during Jesus' arrest. "Jesus commanded Peter, 'Put your sword away! Shall I not drink the cup the Father has given me?'" (John 18:11). Likewise, when Jesus encountered the woman caught in adultery, He had the authority, both as a Jew and as the Son of Man, to enforce justice according to the law. Yet, He chose mercy and grace, empowering her to live in alignment with God's Kingdom rather than under societal judgment. "Then neither do I condemn you," Jesus declared. "Go now and leave your life of sin" (John 8:11). We often stop at verse 11, but verse 12 is equally pivotal: "I am the light of the world. Whoever follows me will never walk in darkness, but will have the light of life" (John 8:12).

This passage reveals a vital truth: Jesus, as the visible image of the invisible God (Colossians 1:15), operates from a place of meekness and calls us to do the same.

- ### *The Discerning Heart of Meekness*

Meekness also involves discernment, especially when offering spiritual nourishment to others. Not everyone is ready to receive the deeper truths of God. Just as a parent knows when to give milk instead of meat, meekness enables us to provide what is appropriate for someone's spiritual growth. "I gave you milk, not solid food, for you were not yet ready for it" (1 Corinthians 3:2).

This nurturing approach, guided by the Holy Spirit, requires setting aside personal preferences to seek God's will in ministry. "But when he, the Spirit of truth, comes, he will guide you into all the truth" (John 16:13). By following His lead, we create an environment where others can grow in faith, eventually becoming ready for deeper truths. True spiritual leadership is marked by this humble, nurturing posture.

There is no "junior" Holy Spirit. Whether someone is a child, a new believer, or a mature follower of Christ, they have access to the same Spirit. "For in one Spirit we were all baptized into one body—Jews or Greeks, slaves or free—and all were made to drink of one Spirit" (1 Corinthians 12:13). Still, we must discern when to offer milk and when to serve meat. Think of it like a refrigerator—you need to know when to grab the milk, scoop out the ice cream, or pull out a steak.

- *Generosity of Spirit*

Meekness is also characterized by a generous spirit. It's about serving others, not out of need, lack, or personal gain, but from an overflow of grace. When we approach life with open hands—ready to give our time, talents, and resources—we embody the essence of meekness. This giving doesn't deplete us; instead, it multiplies what we have. In God's economy, generosity begets generosity, creating a cycle of blessing that enriches both giver and receiver. "Give, and it will be given to you. A good measure, pressed down, shaken together, and running over, will be poured into your lap. For with the measure you use, it will be measured to you" (Luke 6:38).

While often applied to finances, this principle extends far beyond money. It encompasses everything we have to offer the body of Christ. "Freely you have received; freely give" (Matthew 10:8).

Generosity within the body of Christ fosters unity and collaboration rather than competition. When we engage others from a place of meekness, we cultivate unity and collaboration rather than competition. "Make every effort to keep the unity of the Spirit through the bond of peace" (Ephesians 4:3). In this atmosphere, God's authority can move freely, paving the way for lasting revival and cultivating spiritual growth.

By embracing meekness, we align with our true identity in Christ. "Therefore, as God's chosen people, holy and dearly loved, clothe yourselves with compassion, kindness, humility, gentleness, and patience" (Colossians 3:12). Through meekness, we reflect God's heart and invite others to experience His transformative love.

- *Meekness in the Context of Revival*

Meekness is foundational for revival. True revival is not born of human effort but is a move of the Holy Spirit— bringing dead things back to life as God intended. It demands a collective posture of humility and surrender, relinquishing personal agendas to embrace God's purposes, even when they challenge our understanding. "Humble yourselves before the Lord, and he will lift you up" (James 4:10).

Meekness invites us to face new challenges within God's family with open hearts, acknowledging that His ways are higher than ours. "For my thoughts are not your thoughts, neither are your ways my ways," declares the Lord. "As the heavens are higher than the earth, so are my ways higher than your ways and my thoughts than your thoughts" (Isaiah 55:8-9). By cultivating this humility, we create space for God to move freely, drawing others into the revival experience as we embody His love and grace. When meekness becomes a way of life, it nurtures a culture of revival, not just a moment of it.

- *The Divine Mystery of Authority*

At the heart of meekness lies a profound mystery: in God's kingdom, true authority is found not in exerting control but in surrendering it to Him. When we relinquish our desire for power, we gain access to the greater authority that comes from God. Jesus said, "Whoever wants to become great among you must be your servant, and whoever wants to be first must be your slave—just as the Son of Man did not come to be served, but to serve" (Matthew 20:26-28).

This divine paradox reveals that true authority comes through servanthood, empowering us to be instruments of God's will. In surrendering to Him, we find strength, reflecting the meekness of Christ, who, though all-powerful, chose to submit to the Father's will.

- *The Path of True Dominion*

Meekness is not passive; it is an active choice to live out our faith authentically. By embracing meekness, we recognize our authority as God's children and choose to surrender that authority in service to others. In doing so, we find true dominion—not through control but through the transformative power of meekness. Jesus reminds us, "Blessed are the meek, for they will inherit the earth" (Matthew 5:5).

As we cultivate meekness, we allow the Holy Spirit to lead us, becoming vessels of God's mercy, grace, and love. This journey mirrors the example of Christ, who, despite possessing all authority, walked the path of humility and service.

- ### *The Meekness of Christ as Our Model*

Jesus is the ultimate example of meekness. Though He had divine authority, He chose to serve rather than be served. "Take my yoke upon you and learn from me, for I am gentle and humble in heart, and you will find rest for your souls" (Matthew 11:29). His humility and compassion were evident in every aspect of His life, from His birth in a stable to His interactions with the marginalized and outcast.

Even in the face of hostility and suffering, Jesus displayed meekness. When He was reviled, He did not retaliate; when He suffered, He did not threaten but "entrusted Himself to Him who judges justly" (1 Peter 2:23). This profound example teaches us that true strength is found in gentleness, even amid adversity.

- ### *Meekness in Leadership*

Meekness in leadership may seem counterintuitive in a world that often values assertiveness and dominance. However, biblical leadership flips this notion on its head. Leaders who embody meekness inspire trust and loyalty.

Proverbs 16:32 reminds us: "Better a patient person than a warrior, one with self-control than one who takes a city."

Meek leaders prioritize the needs of others, fostering collaboration and growth. By valuing input and empowering others to contribute their gifts, they cultivate a culture of dignity and respect. This kind of leadership results in lasting impact and unity within the community.

- *Meekness and Conflict Resolution*

In times of conflict, meekness allows us to approach disagreements with humility and a desire for reconciliation. "A gentle answer turns away wrath, but a harsh word stirs up anger" (Proverbs 15:1). Instead of seeking to win an argument, meekness encourages us to prioritize understanding and healing.

When we handle conflict with meekness, we reflect Christ's love, creating opportunities for restoration and peace. This approach doesn't avoid difficult conversations but engages them with grace, seeking resolution rather than division.

- *The Transformative Power of Meekness*

Meekness has the power to transform not only individual relationships but entire communities. When God's people embody meekness, they become a powerful witness to the world, demonstrating the redemptive power of Christ. "Do nothing out of selfish ambition or vain conceit. Rather, in humility value others above yourselves" (Philippians 2:3).

In a culture that often prioritizes self-promotion, the meekness of God's people serves as a counter-narrative, showing that true strength lies in love and service. This shift can draw others to the gospel, revealing Christ through our actions and attitudes.

- ***Meekness as a Catalyst for Change***

Meekness can serve as a catalyst for change, both personally and in the broader culture. By surrendering our desires and ambitions, we create space for God's transformative power to manifest. "For the Lord takes delight in his people; he crowns the humble with victory" (Psalm 149:4).

In moments of injustice or hardship, meekness compels us to seek solutions rooted in love and justice. By standing with the vulnerable and advocating for the oppressed, we reflect God's heart for righteousness. This meekness becomes a powerful force for change, leading others to experience the hope and healing found in Christ.

- ***Cultivating Meekness in Our Lives***

To cultivate meekness, we must deepen our relationship with God through prayer and meditation on His Word. "He guides the humble in what is right and teaches them his way" (Psalm 25:9). Biblical literacy is essential for cultivating meekness. Seeking God's heart within His Word, as well as in prayer and worship, fosters gratitude, service, and humility—shaping us into His likeness.

- **The Fruits of Meekness**

The fruits of meekness manifest as greater peace, purpose, and unity in our relationships. "The fruit of the Spirit is love, joy, peace, forbearance, kindness, goodness, faithfulness, gentleness, and self-control" (Galatians 5:22-23). By embodying meekness, we align with God's will, experiencing deeper spiritual growth filled with the fruit of the Spirit.

- **Conclusion: Embracing Meekness for True Dominion**

Meekness is not a sign of weakness but a demonstration of strength rooted in humility, love, and service. By surrendering control to God, we allow Him to work through us, shaping our lives for His glory. "God opposes the proud but shows favor to the humble" (James 4:6).

Let us embrace meekness as the key to true dominion, reflecting God's heart and advancing His kingdom. Through meekness, we unlock a deeper relationship with God and a more authentic expression of our faith, leading to lasting transformation.

CHAPTER ELEVEN

—————————•••••◦‹≪›•••••—————————

ACCOUNTABILITY

—————————•••••◦‹≪›•••••—————————

In the prophetic world, let alone the realm of ministry, accountability is one of the most vital yet often neglected components of a healthy spiritual life. It's a topic frequently discussed but rarely implemented effectively. For those called to serve, teach, equip, and lead, accountability is not merely a recommendation—it's a lifeline. I firmly believe there is no such thing as too much accountability; however, there is such a thing as the wrong type of accountability. Later in this chapter, we'll explore how to identify the right individuals to include in your accountability circle. But first, let's delve into what biblical accountability truly entails and why it is indispensable.

If you examine pastors, prophets, leaders, and ministers who have stumbled, fallen into immorality, or compromised their integrity, a common thread emerges: a lack of healthy, biblical accountability and/or an elevation of authority to the point where they answer to no one. Often, these individuals had little to no accountability, or they believed they had accountability, but it was superficial and far from what they truly needed.

Surface-level check-ins or casual conversations are insufficient to build a safeguard around one's heart, mind, and spirit.

The kind of accountability we are addressing involves deeper relationships with increased attentiveness based on biblical principles—a commitment among believers to encourage one another to live in alignment with Scripture. Biblical accountability is not merely about pointing out flaws; it is about building each other up, creating spaces for honesty and vulnerability, and fostering spiritual growth. It involves mutual responsibility to support, guide, and, when necessary, challenge one another.

Accountability is more than reporting actions or behaviors; it's about building relationships grounded in trust and mutual growth. A truly biblical accountability partnership is built on these principles:

1. Honesty and Transparency: To be accountable to someone, you have to be willing to be vulnerable and trust that that vulnerability will not be used against you. This means being open about struggles, temptations, and weaknesses with trusted individuals. It's not easy to admit our failings, but biblical accountability requires us to bring these to the light with people we trust. In doing so, we prevent sin from growing in secrecy and isolation. As prophetic people, this is super hard for us. We struggle here because of a couple of reasons. These encounters we have are intense most of the time, so most of the time it feels bigger than us. So why would we need to filter these through my accountability relationships? The second one is we tend to be rejected, so we are afraid of rejection for our faults.

I recently heard a pastor of a very well-respected church in Alabama speak on this topic as he was reviewing his time within this ministry network that they were trying to sell me on being a part of. Something struck me deep to my core. He said, "I now have someone that I can share my deepest faults or sins with. I have never been able to share with people in my life or ministry, as it would damn me in their eyes, and I would lose the trust in the church. Not everyone is mature enough for me to trust them with being vulnerable. But with these people, I trust and am accountable to, I can pull off my armor and show them my scars.

They, in turn, take their armor off and show me the same scars. They help me overcome and heal from these wounds within victory; through Jesus, they have won in the same area. Those painful areas are less and less as I get more vulnerable with these trusted people." I couldn't describe this principle better than this man of God's quote. I was rocked to the core. This is it.

2.   Encouragement and Support: Accountability isn't just about correction; it's also about support. We all need encouragement to stay the course, to remain faithful, and to grow stronger in our prophetic walk. This support can come in the form of a prayer partner, a mentor, or a small prophetic group that prays and encourages one another through the highs and lows of life. Cheerleaders are one of the most overlooked types of people we need to keep around us. When times are tight, we don't need people on the island with us. We need people on the opposite beach cheering us on to swim into those deep waters of God's goodness. Keep those people that are so positive it almost makes you annoyed. I have a few of those, and man, are they amazing and deeply needed!

3.   Loving Correction: True accountability involves lovingly confronting one another when we stray off course. This doesn't mean condemning but rather offering correction with compassion. Proverbs 27:17 says, "As iron sharpens iron, so one person sharpens another." This sharpening process is not always comfortable, but it's necessary for our growth and maturity. I have had a few times in my life when the closest accountability person and the closest person to me outside of my wife would just show up at my house and tell me I needed to take a break. Take your wife and go on a date and relax. And he and his wife watch our kids. I cannot tell you how much that has changed my life. He rebuked me when I was speaking negatively about myself a few times. We all need someone like that. He has changed my life in so many ways. He is trustworthy and honest to a fault. He doesn't want anything from me but wants everything for me. He is humble, and he has years of walking with ministers. He has a long history of walking with the Spirit of God. All those things I believe are a prerequisite for a good accountability mentor.

4.   Regular Touchpoints: Consistency is key in any accountability relationship. Having regular check-ins, whether weekly or monthly, creates a rhythm that keeps everyone engaged and mindful of their commitments. These meetings don't have to be long, and I don't think they should be formal, but they should be intentional, covering each person's spiritual journey, challenges, and progress. These cannot become robotic or a box we check. They have to be foundationally based on your relationship with each other first and foremost.

5.   Responsibility to Each Other: Biblical accountability requires us to take responsibility for each other's spiritual well-being. James 5:16 urges us to "confess your sins to one another and pray for one another, that you may be healed." This responsibility calls for a deep commitment to each other's growth, healing, and faithfulness. Galatians 6:2 calls us to carry each other's burdens. This has to be a two-way street. This cannot be just an authoritative relationship. This has to be a back-and-forth relationship. One should not benefit from the relationship in a way that the other side doesn't also benefit. There has to be a servant's heart within both towards each other. I have personally experienced and witnessed where this was not the case. It caused hurt, distrust, and resistance to wanting real accountability. So this is where we need to be careful and prayerfully choose our accountability people..

In life and ministry, it is crucial for prophetic people to have accountability because we often face unique pressures and temptations. The very nature of leadership can sometimes lead people to a place of isolation or loneliness, which is a breeding ground for compromise. Without accountability, it's easy for small compromises to grow into significant issues, eventually leading to moral or ethical failures. When prophetic people are accountable to others, they are reminded that they don't walk this journey alone and that there are people who genuinely care about their well-being.

Prophets and prophetic people who fall often had what they thought was accountability, but it was not the kind of accountability that truly protects. Real accountability isn't afraid to ask hard questions, address uncomfortable topics, or hold someone to the high standards of integrity and godly living. Real accountability carries and understands Proverbs 4:23, where it says: "Above all else, guard your heart, for everything you do flows from it."Help me guard my heart, and I'll help you guard yours.

Now that we've discussed what biblical accountability entails, let's talk about the importance of choosing the right people to be accountable to. Not everyone can serve as an effective accountability partner. Choosing the wrong people—whether due to a lack of spiritual maturity, trustworthiness, or understanding—can do more harm than good.

Here are some guidelines for selecting the right people for accountability:

1. Seek Spiritual Maturity: Look for individuals who have a deep and mature relationship with God. This should be someone who has been walking with the Holy Spirit for a significant amount of time. I would not suggest someone with a new or relatively recent walk with the Lord. These individuals should understand the importance of accountability and be able to approach it with wisdom and discernment.

2. Choose Trustworthy Individuals: Accountability requires honesty and vulnerability, so it's crucial to choose people you can trust. Trustworthy individuals will keep your conversations confidential and won't judge or condemn you for your struggles. This is essential when letting people into your inner circle of life. They are going to see your mess, and you're going to see theirs. We need people to protect us just as much as we need to protect them as we work through things.

3.   Prioritize Those Who Will Challenge You: True accountability partners won't just tell you what you want to hear. They will challenge you to grow and lovingly confront you when you're drifting off course. Avoid people who are likely to take a passive role or who fear addressing uncomfortable topics. A "Yes Man" is not good for anyone. This is especially important for prophets and prophetic people. We need individuals who can say, "That word you gave or vision you had seems off. Here's what I'm discerning about it." It's crucial to find people who can handle these situations with compassion while also being firm. Mishandling such matters can lead to mistrust and unnecessary problems, so choose someone who is skilled at addressing tough topics with care.

4.   Look for People Who Will Pray for You: Accountability isn't just about conversations; it's also about intercession. Seek people who will genuinely pray for you, lifting you up for strength, wisdom, and spiritual growth. I've found that a key trait to look for is someone who prays for you without feeling the need to announce it. When this calling to accountability is genuine, it won't come with an expectation of recognition. This, for me, is a significant indicator of whether someone is the right fit as an accountability partner.

In a world that often encourages independence and self-reliance, the church is called to foster a culture of mutual accountability and encouragement. Biblical accountability helps us stay faithful to our calling and grounded in our relationship with God. It's about more than just avoiding sin—it's about becoming more like Christ and helping others do the same. For prophets and prophetic people, this takes on an even greater importance, as we need to remain rooted in community and avoid the tendencies toward isolation or self-reliance.

If we want to see healthier, stronger prophets and prophetic communities among God's children, we need to prioritize biblical accountability in our lives and ministries. Accountability isn't a sign of weakness; it's a sign of wisdom and humility. By embracing accountability, we acknowledge our need for others on this journey and honor God by committing to live in a way that reflects His love and truth.

CHAPTER TWELVE

FOUNDATIONAL RELATIONSHIPS

One of the most challenging issues within our community is developing and maintaining the right relationships. When chosen carefully, these relationships have the potential to accelerate our growth and provide a solid foundation of support. They encourage, empower, and, as my wife says, "smooth out our rough edges."

While this topic is relevant to all believers, this chapter will focus primarily on prophets. However, even if you are not called to the prophetic office, do not skip this section— many principles shared here are applicable to all followers of Christ.

Prophets, you may find this lesson uncomfortable. The relationships we need most are often the hardest to cultivate because they are frequently with people who view the world and Scripture differently than we do. In many church contexts, we may struggle to understand or relate to these individuals.

I believe it is necessary to clarify the fivefold ministry, as it has been understood within the Western Church. This topic has been explored extensively, but I will approach it from a fresh perspective, offering what I hope will be greater clarity to this sometimes perplexing concept.

Very early in my spiritual journey, the Lord began speaking to me about the fivefold ministry. My salvation came through a radical encounter with the living God. Within a week, I found myself captivated by Ephesians 4—it became a "trap" I couldn't escape for years. What a beautiful trap it was, designed by the Lord to refine and shape me during that wonderful season.

To condense this to its essence: apostles establish and transform culture. Their primary purpose is to convert any culture they encounter into the culture of the Kingdom of God. Apostles are often mistaken for church planters, but this is a misunderstanding. While they may plant churches, that is not their primary role or calling. Their mission is to prepare the saints to bring the Kingdom of Heaven wherever they go.

The term "apostle" itself is derived from a Roman context. Roman apostles were sent to newly conquered territories to make them resemble Rome in every way. They served as cultural architects, ensuring that these territories reflected the values, appearance, and atmosphere of Rome. Similarly, fivefold apostles carry the culture of Heaven, transforming every place they touch to mirror the Kingdom of God.

Prophets, on the other hand, serve as God's mouthpieces. Their role is to help others hear God's voice for themselves. They prepare the saints to proclaim messages of edification and exhortation, bringing light to dark places. Prophets are often more focused on what is coming than on what is happening. They see the gold hidden in those living in darkness and are led by God's voice to reveal that they are known and loved by their Heavenly Father.

Shepherds, or pastors, prepare the saints through healing and reconciliation. They embody Christ as the Redeemer, protecting the flock and nurturing its growth. Shepherds are family-oriented and patient, often serving as the gentle touch of God's grace in the Body of Christ. They mature and prepare believers to fulfill their individual callings, guiding them with compassion and care.

Teachers are critical, particularly for prophets and prophetic people. Prophets need teachers to ground them. Teachers serve as the fivefold ministry's "Supreme Court," filtering everything through the Word of God. Spirit-filled and Spirit-led, they prepare believers to discern all things by Scripture. A true fivefold teacher can transform lives, helping prophets balance their inclination to act quickly with the wisdom of thorough study. This foundational role is indispensable for equipping the Body of Christ.

Lastly, we have evangelists, who equip believers to share Christ with the world. While they may actively preach the gospel, their primary role is to prepare others to do the same. Evangelists empower the Body of Christ to bring the good news to all corners of the earth.

Each of the fivefold ministries is called to equip the saints—no more, no less. Other tasks may arise within these functions, but their foremost purpose is to prepare others to the point where they are no longer dependent on them. This is often a challenging reality to accept.

There was a season when I wrestled with confidence in the ministry entrusted to me. The Lord instructed me to examine whether those around me still relied on me or if I had equipped them to hear God's voice for themselves. The call of the fivefold ministry is, and always will be, to equip the saints.

We must keep this truth at the forefront of our ministry. When people begin to rely on us instead of being equipped by us, we must ask the Lord to search our hearts. This reliance runs counter to God's standard for ministry.

Following that foundational section, let us dive deeper: prophets, pastors, and teachers are vital relationships in our lives. I believe these connections are even more critical than having a personal relationship with an apostle. While being connected to apostolic ministry is important for prophetic growth, personal integrity, and our calling, we also need genuine pastors and teachers—those truly anointed by God for these offices, not just anyone in the church pulpit.

In prophetic circles, communities, and conferences, we are often taught—at least I was—that pastors dislike the prophetic ministry. While there is some truth to this, as previously discussed, we in the prophetic ministry have not always been the best stewards or communicators. The responsibility for this tension lies with both pastors and prophets.

The pastoral office is particularly crucial for prophets because it centers on healing and reconciliation, which are foundational to all other ministry. In Scripture, the pastor is likened to a shepherd, someone who protects the flock and tends to their wounds. Pastors focus on family and restoration, often excelling in hospitality and in gathering believers together. This is especially important for prophets, who can feel isolated, like Elijah in 1 Kings 19. Prophets often feel alone in their calling, but the truth is we are not alone. The Body of Christ not only loves prophets but also values those who equip them. Surrounding ourselves with faithful pastors can provide a spiritual home and remind us to leave behind the isolation of our proverbial caves.

In my view, the most crucial relationship for a prophet is with their teacher. Teachers are anchors in a prophet's life, grounding us in biblical literacy, which is an essential issue in prophetic communities and the broader church. Without these connections, prophets can become so consumed by spiritual encounters that they lose their connection to the community of Christ. I have learned the importance of presenting my words and revelations to teachers, allowing them to sift through and filter them with the wisdom of the Word. Praise God for the gift of teaching! Teachers do more than instruct from a pulpit—they ignite a hunger for God's Word in our hearts. Time and time again, I have gained clarity and understanding about a revelation I received simply by consulting a teacher. Their role is indispensable.

A healthy prophet will have strong relationships with pastors and teachers. These should form the foundation of a prophet's self-imposed accountability. Learn from my mistakes—I once ran my ministry without these relationships, and it was detrimental.

In the past, I often clashed with teachers and pastors. I would stubbornly defend the revelations I received from the spiritual realm, resisting when they saw things differently or suggested alternate paths. Over time, I came to understand and respect their perspectives. Today, I have immense appreciation for their roles and their wisdom.

Most prophetic individuals can be like bulls in a china shop—charging ahead with revelations and making messes for pastors to clean up. While not all prophets are this way, it is common for us to focus so much on receiving downloads and encounters from God that we overlook the responsibility of stewarding these gifts within the Body of Christ and the broader community.

This brings us to the concept of "WWH" (Who, What, How). We must approach this concept with a spirit of honor. Honor, in biblical terms, means "to take at weight." When we honor someone, we recognize their worth and value. To curse someone is to treat them lightly, disregarding the fact that Christ died for them and considers them priceless. Often, we confuse honor with respect. While both are important, honor is foundational— it is impossible to love without honor.

Prophets, we must honor pastors and teachers. Jesus Himself honors their calling and purpose. We are called to serve and submit to their leadership. The fivefold ministry is not a hierarchy to be wielded for power; it is a unified system, much like the Trinity. Just as the Trinity functions in harmony, the fivefold ministries are meant to operate together. One without the others is incomplete. Any attempt to function with just one or two ministries while neglecting the others is ineffective.

Prophets, serve pastors and teachers. Serve apostles and evangelists. Honor them. Respect them. Love them. Submit to their God-given authority. Even within the Trinity, there is delegated authority, and the same principle applies to the fivefold ministry.

If we approach these relationships with humility and gentleness, submitting to God's authority, we will walk in honor. Walking in honor opens the door to love and favor, which positions us to serve our communities in ways we cannot imagine.

Honor is the key to the prophet's calling! It is the lens through which we view humanity because God values them so highly, and we must do the same.

CHAPTER THIRTEEN

———— ••••◈•••• ————

THE WEIGHT

———— ••••◈•••• ————

I t's strange as I look back on my life. When I was in high school and college, I was doing everything to gain weight. I was working out, eating, drinking protein shakes, and doing whatever I could to put on weight. I was, as the kids say, "trying to get swole." Then I hit my 30s, and I started doing everything I could to keep the weight off while maintaining my muscle mass. It's funny to me how my perspective and drive have shifted regarding such a basic thing.

I've talked with many guys who agree this is a normal shift in men's minds. Weight is such a huge focus in our culture here in the United States. Typically, women aim to get or stay smaller, while men often want to get bigger in their younger years. But what if we focused on the weight that truly matters?

To take someone or something at their "weight" is the biblical definition of honor. The opposite of honor is cursing, which means taking something lightly or treating someone or something as lesser in value than how it was created.

Weight is one of the greatest revelations we, as the body of Christ—especially prophetic people—need to understand! We need to see, perceive, and take people at their God-given weight. We must recognize how much weight people carry in God's eyes and treat them accordingly. Weight! What an incredible concept!

But what if I perceive someone's weight as less than it truly is? That's called cursing. To curse someone is to take or treat them as having less value or weight than they possess. For instance, when God cursed nations in the Old Testament, He essentially dismissed them: "Yeah, that's just the Moabites..." He took them lightly, which obviously is something you for sure do not want.

Why am I exploring this concept of cursing and honoring? It's twofold:

1. We must diligently see and treat everyone and everything around us with the value or weight God sees in them. This must be a high priority!

2. Even more importantly, we need to honor ourselves and see the weight and value God has placed in us. This is paramount. It has to be the focus of every prophetic person and the body of Christ at large. Since this book is for prophets and prophetic people, let's zero in on us.

Let's be honest: prophets and prophetic people are often on an emotional roller coaster. We feel more deeply than most. If you've seen the movie Avatar, it offers a great analogy. When the Na'vi say, "I see you," it conveys a deep connection with the love and honor of those around them. This is similar to how prophets and prophetic people typically operate. When I saw that movie for the first time, I heard, clear as day, "This is how I created the heart of the prophet."

We see and feel more than most people walking this planet. We hurt deeper, love deeper, and are passionate about things others don't understand. We feel beaten down and don't know why. We get excited about things before others see the fruit we are excited about. Our highs are high, and our lows are low. This is the typical life I've observed over the years, both in myself and in others running in prophetic circles. For those who don't struggle with this—PRAISE GOD! I've met only a few like that, but I know they exist. Still, it's not the norm.

So, is this just the burden of prophetic people? Is this simply the way it is? Is this our thorn in the flesh, the rock we must carry, the suffering we are called to endure?

I can't be the only one who has wrestled with these questions. The answer is yes and no—it all comes down to perspective. Stay with me on this journey, and I promise it will be freeing for us!

The first part of the answer is yes: it is the prophetic call to carry this burden and endure this suffering. We have been gifted and graced with the privilege of feeling what God feels and what those around us feel. We have the privilege of bearing the weight of others' burdens (Galatians 6:2). We are privileged to lose sleep interceding for people and situations. We are blessed to endure attacks from the enemy because the gifts God has given us hold tremendous value to Him. The enemy hates the prophetic because it is one of God's greatest gifts.

Hearing the voice of God is the one thing that Satan does not want. His sole plan is to stop you from building a relationship with God. It's impossible to have a relationship without two-way communication between both parties. The struggles are still real, though. They still happen.

Does it hurt? Is it exhausting? Yes, at times. But should it dictate or change our actions as we move forward in the purpose for which we were created? Absolutely not!

The weight we carry as prophetic people is heavy. It represents something Satan himself hates with every fiber of his fallen being. We are neon signs pointing to the amazing purpose each individual uniquely carries. We get to call out what is unseen to be seen. We are called to pull out the image of God within people for the world to see. This is everything Satan longed for when he was in heaven. We embody what he desired but will never have—not just as prophets and prophetic people but as the entire human race.

However, we are not called to suffer simply because we are prophetic. The prophetic is not something to be endured but cherished. As Paul says, "Pursue love, yet earnestly desire spiritual gifts, but especially that you may prophesy" (1 Corinthians 14:1). He wouldn't encourage us to seek something earnestly if it was meant to be a burden that ruins our joy, quality of life, or relationships.

So where is the disconnect? Why do so many in the prophetic community experience these struggles regularly?

First and foremost, we do not understand our own weight, let alone the weight of others. Satan longed to be like God, but God created us in His image instead. We are the one thing Satan desires desperately but can never be or have. For centuries, we've been taught that Satan's goal is to deceive, cause us to sin, and steal, kill, and destroy. While this is true, it's not the full picture. Satan's torment comes from seeing us—beings made in the image of God—walking out our purpose and calling.

If God is a good Father, He would never send His children into harm's way. Just as we would never drop our kids off in a drug-infested house, God wouldn't send us into the world to be tormented by Satan without purpose or protection. Instead, He has given us authority to triumph over darkness and bring the fullness of His image to light. We are here to torment Satan, not the other way around. The tables have been turned, starting in Genesis 1; we've just had a bad perspective.

God is a good Father. He is filled with wisdom and love, always wanting the best for us. When we doubt this truth, we must take those thoughts captive and reject them. Sin is missing the mark—believing a thought God does not have. Jesus taught this when He said, "Anyone who even looks at a woman with lust has already committed adultery with her in his heart" (Matthew 5:28). This is less about the action and more about the thought behind it.

If our minds are renewed in Christ, we should think His thoughts. When we take ourselves at the weight God has given us as His children, our thoughts will align with His. From there, it becomes easier to honor the weight of everyone we encounter.

Honor is the currency of the Kingdom of God. Love is its foundation, walls, and atmosphere, but honor is the currency we invest in people through love, bringing exponential growth and blessings to them.

Let us be people who view weight as a lens of honor, equipping the saints to hear the voice of their Father and treat others with the value He sees in them.

CHAPTER FOURTEEN

---•••••<❖>••••••---

WOUNDED PROPHET DISEASE

---•••••<❖>••••••---

T his chapter is particularly dear to my heart, as it touches on an area where I have the most personal experience. It resonates deeply with me, and I firmly believe it addresses one of the most pressing topics needing greater exploration within the body of Christ. Prophets and prophetic individuals, let's have an honest conversation—this is a safe space for us.

As prophetic people, we often embody a whirlwind of emotions, navigating the highs and lows of a spiritual roller coaster. We feel deeply. We see deeply. We hear deeply. At times, this depth can profoundly impact our emotions, perceptions, life choices, relationships, and even marriages. It's a challenge not only for us as individuals but also for the communities we are part of.

But let me be clear—this emotional turbulence is not the purpose or calling we are meant to sustain. Many of us have been taught that this is simply the "burden" of being prophetic, a weight we must carry. Elijah's life in the Bible has often been held as the standard of what we will endure as prophets and prophetic people. However, that teaching is far from the truth. We are not condemned to a life of suffering, even though suffering for Christ is an undeniable part of the Christian journey. We are talking about two different things here. The New Testament mentions suffering 22 times, affirming that following Christ comes with its challenges and its own suffering for the gospel. Yet, the suffering I am speaking of here, in regard to prophets and prophetic people, is different.

The struggles often labeled by the world as "depression" are, unfortunately, quite common among prophets and prophetic people. We are often hesitant to confront or even acknowledge these struggles. How can we possibly battle depression when, as Christians, we're told we shouldn't be dealing with it—especially as individuals so intimately connected to the Spirit? As a result, we often hide it. We don't talk about it. We tell others we're fine when we're not. We minister to people while inwardly falling apart. Our intense focus on the heavenly and the voice of God sometimes leads us to neglect our own well-being here on earth.

This, however, is not our calling. We are not meant to be tossed about by our emotions. We are not called to live under the weight of constant negativity, depression, or anger. It's not normal or acceptable for those around us to feel discouraged or drained by our presence. If that's the case, it's a clear sign we need to pause and look inward.

We are not called to see only the negative in people or institutions, nor are we meant to live in a perpetual state of frustration, anger, or apathy. The image of the grumpy prophet, groaning and grumbling at the back of the church week after week, is not who we are meant to be.

Instead, we are called to live lives filled with joy—one-third of the kingdom of God! The other two-thirds are righteousness (discussed in Chapter 2) and peace. This means our thoughts, actions, and entire being should be rooted in the peace that comes from being the righteousness of Christ, while overflowing with joy. If we are missing one of them, we are missing a massive piece of what the Bible confirms makes up the kingdom of God (Romans 14:17). This has to be the standard and the filter through which we continually view our earthly and spiritual lives.

Let's reject the notion that emotional chaos is our destiny. Instead, let us embrace the fullness of our calling: to be carriers of joy, peace, and righteousness, encouraging everyone wherever we go by prophesying redemption and hope, all while equipping the saints to the fullness of Christ.

What is this prophetic depression exactly? Where does it come from, and why is it so common among prophets and prophetic individuals? How do we combat it?

I'm so glad you asked. These are the exact questions we need to address—not just to fight against this issue but to understand its nature, origins, and how to recognize it when it's coming, so we can prepare for it. We also need to tackle this epidemic head-on in our prophetic communities, dismantling the lies and building ourselves up with truth.

A prime example from scripture comes to mind—the life of Elijah. Elijah is one of the most well-known prophets, and his experiences are incredibly relatable for anyone walking in the prophetic. God allowed us to see Elijah's struggles and emotional highs and lows, giving us a window into what many of us go through.

Every prophetic person has likely studied Elijah's life in depth, and for good reason. After mastering the basics of the prophetic—especially as it's explained under the new covenant—I would recommend every prophetic person start by studying Elijah.

I want to share an important insight with everyone: it's absolutely vital to read scripture through a historical, contextual, and covenantal lens. We cannot approach the entire Bible as though it was written under the New Covenant or based on the realities we live in today. Understanding the different covenants is essential to interpreting and applying scripture truthfully.

Familiarizing yourself with the five major covenants, their placement in scripture, and the cultural and historical context of the time when they were written is transformative. This perspective brings incredible clarity and truth. When I began studying scripture this way, it unlocked so much revelation for me and has been an invaluable tool in my spiritual journey in the prophetic and my biblical understanding.

Now, let's get back to Elijah. He faced intense emotional ups and downs, battled doubt and a lack of faith, was hated by people, and had many enemies. Yet, despite these challenges, he accomplished incredible things. He witnessed healings, delivered accurate prophetic words, and boldly displayed the power of God in extraordinary ways. But these victories didn't come easily—they came through perseverance and trust in God.

This does not need to be the norm for us. We have been fed a lie that this is what we must deal with. We have believed that this is just part of the call, the thorn in our side we have to bear. But the more I studied Elijah, I realized he was just a man called to be a prophet who had some major identity problems.

Elijah had moments of little faith and significant doubt. At times, he isolated himself socially, withdrawing from others. We often look at prophets in the Bible—Elijah especially—and see them as larger than life, more anointed, and having a greater calling than ourselves or those around us. And let's be honest, Elijah did some incredible things. From my perspective, God tasked him with foundational, groundbreaking roles for the prophetic that still serve as a guide for us today.

In many ways, I think of Elijah as the oldest brother in the family of office prophets. As the oldest brother, he had to find his way in uncharted territory, walking a path no one had tread at the level he did. He was, in a sense, a pioneer. And pioneers often make more mistakes than others because they are building the road as they walk it. These mistakes, however, serve as lessons for those who follow. That, I believe, is one of Elijah's greatest purposes for us. His struggles should not become our struggles. They should not justify lifestyles below what Jesus paid for on the cross. Instead, we should learn from his mistakes and grow because of them.

How amazing is it that God included Elijah's full story in the Bible—the victories, the struggles, the shortcomings— so we can both marvel at his achievements and gain wisdom from his errors? It is an incredible blessing to prophets and prophetic people today.

Let's explore some of the shortcomings in Elijah's ministry and address what we can learn from them. At the end, I'll share the most transformative thing God gave Elijah, which shifted everything for him and is available to us today, enabling us to run the prophetic race well.

Elijah's Shortcomings

1. Using God-given authority out of insecurity and pain rather than for its intended purpose (2 Kings 2:23–24).

Though this passage pertains to Elisha rather than Elijah, it offers a key learning moment for prophetic individuals. Elisha had just lost his mentor, Elijah—a father figure—and was deeply mourning. Adding to this, Elisha, a young man in his mid-twenties, was now shouldering the immense mantle of prophetic responsibility for the first time. When he encountered a group of boys mocking him, it became the proverbial straw that broke the camel's back.

This situation underscores an important lesson: we must not use our gifts or authority as a reaction to personal pain or frustration. Our words carry immense power—they bring life or death. Additionally, we must be mindful of the example we set, especially in tough times.

Reading between the lines, it's plausible Elisha had observed Elijah's insecurities and shortcomings, particularly under pressure. He likely saw Elijah occasionally react impulsively rather than with wisdom. Similarly, we've all had moments of reacting out of pain or frustration, saying things we later regret. Perhaps, like me, you've even "prophesied" from a place of hurt rather than from God's truth.

This highlights the critical need to teach the next generation of prophetic individuals to learn from our mistakes rather than repeat them. Let's model godly wisdom and patience, especially in challenging times.

2. Falling into a "poor me" mindset and questioning God after victories.

Time and again, after God used Elijah in miraculous ways, he fell into despair, lamenting his circumstances and questioning God. This recurring pattern revealed a lack of trust in God's goodness and a shaky understanding of his identity in the Lord.

When my wife and I lost our daughter, Willow, we faced daily choices in our grieving process. We could have blamed God, become angry, or sunk into depression. Instead, we leaned into our understanding of God's goodness, mercy, and peace. Even in the storm, we chose to thank God for the time we had with Willow and rest in His peace.

God did not take our daughter from us. A week after her passing, I stood in the pulpit preaching on the goodness of God, refusing to believe the lie that our storm was His doing. This unwavering trust sustained us. For prophetic individuals, this serves as a vital lesson: trust in God's character, even in the face of adversity.

3. Comparing himself to others and losing focus on his God-given assignment (1 Kings 18–19).

After miraculously defeating 450 prophets, Elijah received a threatening message from Jezebel. In fear, he fled and lamented, "Kill me; I am no better than my fathers."

How could Elijah forget so quickly that God had delivered him from impossible odds? Rather than focusing on God's faithfulness, he spiraled into self-pity, comparing himself to others and measuring his situation by human standards.

Comparison often paralyzes us, just as it paralyzed Elijah. Don't let it freeze you in place. Focus on your unique journey and trust God's process for your life.

4. Blaming others for his struggles.

In 1 Kings 19, Elijah blamed Jezebel for his fear and the Israelites for their unfaithfulness. These external factors became his justification for disobedience and inaction.

We must be careful not to let opposition or challenges keep us stuck. Instead, let resistance propel us higher. As Bill Johnson says, "If you don't run into a demon every once in a while, you're probably going the same way they are." Resistance often signals we're on the right path.

Embrace challenges as opportunities to grow and rise higher with God.

5. Losing faith quickly when God didn't move on his timeline.

In 1 Kings 19, God repeatedly asked Elijah, "Why are you still here?" Despite angelic encounters and clear instructions, Elijah hesitated, paralyzed by fear and doubt.

Little did he know, his best days—filled with companionship and purpose alongside Elisha—lay ahead. The lesson is clear: stay in faith and joy, expecting great things from God. Don't let fear immobilize you.

6. Exaggerating problems and isolating himself unnecessarily (1 Kings 18:22).

Elijah often lamented that he was the only prophet left, yet Obadiah had hidden 150 prophets from Jezebel.

Isolation magnifies storms, making them seem insurmountable. The truth is, most of us face similar struggles, and we are never called to walk this prophetic life alone. Surround yourself with a supportive community, even if they don't fully understand your gifting. They can pray, encourage, and offer biblically grounded support.

If you don't have a prophetic community, pray and search for one. Many groups exist, even on social media.

Elijah's story didn't end with his struggles. When God instructed him to mentor Elisha, things began to change. Elijah grew in how he handled situations. Though not perfect, he demonstrated significant growth.

We need "Elijahs" to teach us from their mistakes and "Elishas" whom we can mentor. Surround yourself with people who challenge and encourage you—both as a learner and a teacher.

We cannot let this "wounded prophet disease" infiltrate our community. We must strive to be emotionally and spiritually healthy—not just for ourselves but for the body of Christ and the world we are called to minister to.

When we are wounded, it's hard to reap the harvest we are called to gather. My prayer is that the prophetic community becomes so healthy and unified that we can run at full speed together. Let's rise above the chaos and live out our calling with joy, peace, and righteousness.

CHAPTER FIFTEEN

LANGUAGE OF PASTORS

There is this faraway land of an ancient civilization that goes by the name of pastors. They have this intricate and complex language whose origin does not come from Latin but from the heart of the Father. Archeologists, philologists, and linguists have been studying the language extensively. Philologists have been analyzing ancient texts to try to understand this very perplexing language. It is possibly the eighth wonder of the world to comprehend this unique form of communication.

I'm poking fun here, making light of something that truly reflects my feelings about pastors and the challenge of communicating with them in ways that help them understand—or even want to listen to—the prophets and the prophetic. That's often how I feel, especially in the early years of trying to understand this prophetic calling.

Maybe it's just me, but the more I've talked to other prophets and prophetic people over the years, the more I've realized this experience is very common. Adding to this, many of us have been taught—whether explicitly or implicitly—that pastors are the enemy of the prophetic in some strange way. That they will never agree with the prophetic. That they view us as odd, untrustworthy, and unwilling to give us any opportunities to minister to the people in their churches. They worry we'll harm their congregations. Of course, this is an extremely generalized statement. There are certainly pastors who love and honor the prophetic and welcome it fully. While they are fewer in number compared to those who are less enthusiastic about the prophetic, they exist, and their openness is a blessing. I have a different perspective on this topic than most, so I'll ask for a little grace as I explain my stance.

I believe the tension between pastors and prophetic people stems equally from both sides. Much of the issue lies in how our communication styles fail to be received or understood by the other. I touched on this briefly in the chapter on "cracks," but let's explore this idea a little further.

I'll speak specifically from the perspective of the prophetic toward pastors. I am not a pastor, as my wife continually reminds me during my annual conversation that always starts with, "Let's pastor a church, babe." She quickly smiles, chuckles, and says, "No. You are not a pastor. I didn't marry a pastor; I married a prophet." I've pastored churches, served on church staff and leadership, helped plant churches, advised church leaders, and sat on advisory boards and boards of churches. Through all of that, I learned quickly that I am not a pastor. That's why I have immense respect and honor for pastors. I've been around some great ones, and I've been around some not-so-great ones. I tried to be a pastor, and it was the hardest thing I've ever done. I did some things well and failed at many others. My heart was in the right place, but my ability to function effectively in the pastoral role was lacking. I believe that's why God called me to that season—to teach me. I learned so much about people and pastors: why they do what they do and why I struggled to communicate with them. My hope is that you can learn from my mistakes so you don't have to endure the same hard lessons.

In the prophetic, I've witnessed myself and many others making similar mistakes. Another minister explained this to me in a vivid, almost stomach-turning way, but once I understood it, it made sense. Bear with me, especially if you have a weak stomach. Pray before you read this next part: "Prophetic people often vomit everything they see, sense, and feel. This leaves the rest of us to sift through the mess—deciphering what God has said to you for us—while dealing with the cleanup afterward. It's not only exhausting but also confusing. Most of the time, we don't understand why you're saying it or what to do with it. We struggle to see how it fits into our work of tending to the children of God. We're focused on healing, reconciling, and protecting the flock, so it's hard to connect your words with our mission."

Wow. That hit hard. It hurt deeply until God showed me the truth: He wanted to help me communicate better. He wanted me to avoid leaving pastors to figure out what I had shared and how to incorporate or invest it into the life of the church. Too often, my words were discarded because, from their perspective, deciphering them took too much time. This left me feeling unheard, as though I'd missed the mark. It became easier for them to move on without engaging the prophetic at all, which hurt even more. The thing I was so passionate about—the connection with God that I treasured—was being set aside as though it was worthless. It felt like my heart was being ripped out.

I now believe that the problem lies mostly in our inability to bridge the gap between prophetic language and pastoral language. This is a huge opportunity for us in the prophetic community. I truly believe we hold the key to resolving this disconnect. I also believe we're the majority of the problem—not the pastors. We've been playing the victim card far too long, and it has kept us captive on the fringes of the church.

As a community, we need to stop blaming pastors for excluding the prophetic when we've contributed significantly to that exclusion. I know many of you have experienced pain caused by church leaders. I've been there too. Please hear my heart: I'm not justifying that behavior.

No one, regardless of their role, should hurt others because of their calling or gifting.

I'm writing from that place of pain—the place of being hurt by pastors and leaders in the body of Christ. But I've learned that I can't hold them to standards requiring an understanding they simply don't have. So, I had two choices:

1. Stay angry, hurt, and resentful toward pastors and the church.

2. Seek to understand the disconnect and work toward being part of the solution.

God showed me that the prophetic is good and vital for today. He wants it in the church. He has called prophets to equip the saints. However, when the prophetic is confusing, difficult, messy, or harmful—whether through misuse or unclear communication—it's no wonder many pastors treat it like the plague. Honestly, I probably would too.

When God revealed this to me, I knew I had to change how I communicated to speak the language of pastors. I began to study the pastoral calling: their practices, motivations, and what moves them.

Pastors prepare the saints by healing people and reconciling families within the body of Christ. They shepherd believers to fully embody who Christ is and who they are in Him.

Pastors protect the body of Christ. They are family-focused, often patient with individuals on their spiritual journeys, no matter how slow the progress. They embody God's mercy, maturing and equipping believers to fulfill their callings. They are wonderful mentors who love people deeply. They also struggle with letting go—watching those they've invested in leave the "nest" when they're ready to fly. Pastors often prioritize protection over risk. What a beautiful calling and gifting God has given the church! I'm so thankful for these amazing men and women who live sacrificially, serving the body of Christ day and night. Without their love and care, we would be lost, unable to gather around the table of God's presence as a united body.

So, how do we, prophetic people, communicate with pastors who see through a lens that we don't see through?

I believe this is a multi-layered answer, but it begins with a singular focus that needs to be emphasized above all else: honor. Honor must be the foundation upon which we build all relationships.

The biblical definition of honor is to acknowledge someone or something for its worth—in other words, its value and purpose. Everyone on this planet has value and purpose, or Jesus would not have died for them, even if they haven't accepted Him as their Lord and Savior. They simply may not know their worth or purpose and are thus unable to experience the love of the One who gave them that value.

As children of God, we are called to see people as God sees them and to honor the image of God in which they were created. Pastors are no exception—they deserve immense honor. They are crucial to the body of Christ and hold a special place in the heart of God.

Prophets and prophetic people must start honoring pastors and strive to work with them to fulfill their purpose and calling. We need to serve pastors by building trust so that our gifts can assist in the edification, encouragement, and equipping of the saints through the prophetic, working in unity rather than opposition.

It's vital to understand the importance of filtering things from a flock-to-spiritual-realm standpoint instead of spirit-realm-to-flock. Let me clarify: pastors are deeply focused on the flock—their well-being, health, and families—as the core of their ministry calling. So when they hear anything that doesn't immediately align with what's best for the flock, it's as if they don't hear it. Their senses are tuned to the flock, just as ours, as prophetic people, are tuned to the spiritual realm.

Thank God for that! If pastors weren't focused on the flock, how chaotic would things be if only the prophetic were emphasized? No one would be tended to or ministered to, and families would suffer greatly. Therefore, when we communicate with these incredible pastors, we should share what God reveals to us from a flock-to-Spirit perspective.

We should communicate with clear, simple language, avoiding spiritual jargon that holds little meaning for pastors. Instead, we must emphasize how the message benefits the flock—how it edifies, protects, and supports them. Once delivered, we must allow pastors the authority to decide what to do with the word, with no backlash from us, regardless of how they choose to use or not use it.

We must also stop believing that the prophetic words we receive and deliver are tied to our identity or acceptance within the body of Christ, especially among pastors or people in general. Our role is to deliver the word—not to nurture or act upon it. The focus should be clear and centered on effective delivery.

If we fail to deliver prophetic words in a way pastors can understand, how can we expect them to receive and use the prophetic words effectively? We need to extend mercy to pastors and release the unattainable standard we've placed on ourselves—that every prophetic word we give must be received for us to feel honored.

I deeply believe we should be better janitors than interior designers. Most of the time, we focus on what's happening in the spiritual realm, where God is leading us in the future, and whether there is a catalyst prepared to sustain what we see in the spirit. What we perceive is often what is to come, not what is, and we frequently get so fixated on the future that we grow frustrated with the present reality.

Here's where the mess comes in: constantly speaking about what needs to change can frustrate and undermine everything the pastors have built. Being an interior designer is great, but we also need to recognize when it's time for remodeling and when we simply need to act as janitors and clean up the mess first.

We need to focus on encouraging and edifying what has already been built while also prophesying what is to come. We must be conscious of both and seek the Lord's guidance for both. When we make a mess or miss the mark, we must step into the role of janitor—owning the mess we've created and taking responsibility for cleaning it up.

I recently spoke with a pastor who shared a story about a prophetic woman in his church. She was incredibly gifted but struggled with accountability. When she picked up things in the spirit, she would hide behind the prophetic word, refusing correction. If the word didn't come to pass, she wouldn't take responsibility for missing it.

This is another issue among prophetic people, and I've been guilty of it myself. I've been uncorrectable at times. The better we become at being janitors—owning our mistakes and cleaning them up—the faster pastors will trust us with the prophetic in their churches. Prophets and prophetic people must make the lives of pastors easier, not more difficult. Let's strive to serve pastors with honor and see their calling as God sees it. God loves pastors just as much as prophets and prophetic people—neither more than the other. God has the same honor for both.

I challenge all of us—including myself—to strive to communicate more clearly with pastors moving forward. When pastors and prophets come together in the body of Christ, I believe we will form an unmovable force that cannot and will not be overcome.

CHAPTER SIXTEEN

————•••••◆•••••————

DEAF EARS OR DEAF WORDS

————•••••◆•••••————

❝Every word I give keeps falling on deaf ears" and "I cannot keep throwing pearls before swine" are two statements I frequently hear within prophetic communities. To be honest, I've said those exact words—either privately or to mentors—more times than I'd like to admit. For years, I was super frustrated. That frustration eventually turned into a search for justification. I sought out other prophets and prophetic people who would affirm that we were right and others were wrong.

Then one day, I was listening to a prophet I personally know and respect. On a podcast, he shared how he had struggled with the exact same issue. He said God came to him and revealed that he misunderstood his calling. God told him his calling wasn't to ensure the words he gave were received or came to full maturity. His calling was to minister prophetically to people from a place of edification and exhortation. He had taken on a responsibility that wasn't his to carry.

Hearing this was like having a skyscraper lifted off my chest. I immediately went back to Scripture, as I often do. I couldn't find a single instance where the burden of ensuring a prophetic word came to pass was placed on the prophet. Their responsibility was simply to deliver the word—that was it.

How could I have missed this? This is the simplest lie we, as a prophetic community, have accepted from the pits of hell. We've believed this lie and built a "woe is me" mentality around it, thinking that when people don't receive the words we give as being from God, it's somehow our fault as the deliverers of those words. Our identity as a community is tied up in the reception of the prophetic words and words coming to fullness.

I believe the Lord showed me the origin of this issue within the prophetic community, and it's something that needs to be addressed and removed immediately. I don't believe this idea was introduced with the intention of harm but rather to protect people from going down the wrong path. I also don't believe the root premise is inherently wrong, but the extremes to which it has been taken are problematic.

So, what is it? It's twofold. It begins with the belief in the statement, "Less of me, more of You," paired with the teaching that the gift is not who you are. These ideas need to be examined and understood more clearly to identify where the issue lies.

The phrase "Less of me, more of You" is something I've heard taught in every denomination, church, pastor, minister, and Christian circle. The premise of the statement is well-intentioned, but it's often communicated incorrectly. A more accurate statement would be, "More of me and more of God."

When it's presented as it commonly is, people feel like they must kill who they are and replace themselves with God—as if they are worthless, discarded, and without value. This is entirely anti-gospel. Romans 8 explicitly states that if you are in the flesh, you cannot please God. However, it also clarifies that as followers of Christ, we are not in the flesh but in the Spirit because the Spirit dwells within us. We have zero obligation to the flesh, as it is dead, but we do have an obligation to the Spirit of God.

So while I understand the intention behind the statement and the way it is being said, it causes confusion. Instead, we should seek a greater understanding and awareness of the image of God that dwells within us by His Spirit, as well as an increased awareness of God Himself. Hence, 'More of me, Lord. More of You, God!"

To say "less of us" as people—people who, according to Romans 6, experienced co-death, co-burial, and co-resurrection with Christ—implies that Jesus paid the price on the cross only to deserve less of what He paid for. But Scripture says we are made brand new in Christ, born again. It's time we embrace the full truth of that transformation. We need more of who we are created to be and less of who we were never meant to be. We need a greater understanding and awareness of His Spirit and less focus on battling a flesh that is already dead. We need more understanding of God and deeper awareness of His presence.

Then we move to the other side of the same coin. This next statement must be understood and communicated with much greater clarity: "You are not your gift. Your identity cannot be tied to your gifting."

Prophets, let me speak directly to you: that is a lie from the pits of hell. Jesus gave five gifts to the body of Christ—five types of people. The Apostle, Prophet, Pastor, Teacher, and Evangelist are individuals with unique lenses through which they view the world. They have a distinct, narrow purpose essential for maturing and advancing the body of Christ by equipping the saints.

So, prophets (or any other fivefold ministry office), yes, you are what you are called to be. Prophets, this is who we are. It's not all you are, but it is part of who you are. It is woven into your personality, identity, and how your spirit communicates. Being a prophet is part of your identity. You cannot separate that from yourself, as God knew you before He formed you in your mother's womb (Jeremiah 1:5).

However, the function of the prophet is not the foundation of your identity. While being a prophet is part of your identity, your worth and value are not tied to what you do with being a prophet. If it were possible to remove the prophet from who I am—since I was called to the office of prophet long before I came onto this planet—I would cease to exist. It is woven into everything I do, think, act, am, see, sense, or feel.

For those with prophetic gifting, removing the prophetic from who you are is like taking the mouth, eyes, and ears from your body and expecting you to be the same person. Yet, holding your worth in the prophetic is an entirely different conversation, and I strongly advise against that. To say that the prophetic gift isn't part of your identity negates the truth that the prophetic is part of Christ's identity as the Son of God.

The prophetic gift should never be elevated above the Word of God in Scripture. The Bible is the purest and highest level of prophecy. The entire Word is prophetic, as it is God's Word, and Jesus Himself was the Word made flesh. Therefore, the prophetic was an intrinsic part of Him and His identity.

The problem arises when prophetic people tie their identity to prophesying or being heard. That's where things go wrong. But saying that the gifting itself isn't part of your identity is equally incorrect.

I understand the intention behind the statement, as there has been an issue with people building personal identities around their gifts. When they build their sense of worth on what they can do with the gift rather than on the Giver who empowers it, they stray from the path of righteousness in Christ.

However, we must be careful not to throw the baby out with the bathwater. We need to communicate these truths more clearly, not just repeat statements handed down through tradition. Instead, we should speak truth clearly to combat the lies that have bound the body of Christ— particularly prophetic communities, as they are the ones I am addressing here.

Prophets and prophetic people, the reason we feel as though what we are sharing is equivalent to throwing pearls before swine or falling on deaf ears is that, as a community, we have yet to fully understand who we truly are and what our responsibilities entail.

What you share has nothing to do with who you are or your worth, value, or purpose. What you share is simply seed— no more, no less. Whether or not it grows has little to do with what you are sharing. While communicating effectively, as we've discussed in previous chapters, can increase the likelihood of people receiving the words you give, it doesn't guarantee that those seeds will grow.

For the seed to grow, the soil must be good—and the condition of the soil is not our responsibility. Our responsibility is to deliver the seed. In the parable of the sower (Matthew 13), the seed is spread regardless of the soil's condition. Your identity lies in what kind of soil you are in Christ, not in the seed you are spreading.

So, my fellow prophets and prophetic brothers and sisters, let us be good soil—humble, meek, loving, edifying, and encouraging. Let us prophesy the world back into reconciliation with its Father, returning to the origin of the relationship with the Trinity.

FINAL REFLECTIONS

As we come to the close of Righteous Prophet, it's important to reflect on the journey we've taken together. The life of a prophet is both a privilege and a challenge, filled with moments of divine revelation and opportunities to partner with God's will. It is not a path for the faint of heart but for those willing to trust, obey, and persevere through every trial.

Throughout this book, we have explored the unique struggles that prophets face, along with solutions rooted in Scripture and divine wisdom. Whether it's overcoming strained relationships with pastors, discerning the truth in complex situations, or delivering messages with love and humility, each lesson has been a stepping stone toward fulfilling your prophetic calling with integrity and effectiveness.

But the journey doesn't end here. Walking as a prophet is a lifelong process of growth, refinement, and dependence on God. You will face new challenges and receive new revelations, but with each step, you are being shaped into a vessel that reflects His glory. Never forget that you are not alone in this journey. The same God who called and anointed you is the same God who walks with you every step of the way.

As you move forward, let your life be a testament to the righteousness of God and the transformative power of His word. Stand firm in your calling, seek His guidance in every situation, and remain a humble servant of the one true God.

May this book serve as a continual resource of encouragement and direction as you fulfill your prophetic mission. The world needs your voice, and God has equipped you with everything you need to speak His truth boldly and powerfully.

Now, go forth as a meek prophet, steadfast in purpose, and confident in the One who has called you. The journey continues, but the victory is already assured.

You Are A Righteous Prophet.

ENDNOTES

Vallotton, K. 2014. Basic Training for the Prophetic Ministry. Destiny Image Publishers. (Chapter 4)

Thompson, S. 2010. You May All Prophesy. Morningstar Pubns. (Chapter 4)

Vallotton, K. 2012. Spirit Wars. Chosen Books. (Chapter 6)

Vallotton, K. 2017. Destined To Win. Thomas Nelson Publishing. (Chapter 6)

ABOUT THE AUTHOR

Andrew Phinney is a dedicated servant of God, called to empower and equip prophetic voices for their divine assignments. With a deep passion for prophetic ministry, Andrew has spent years traveling the world, speaking / ministering in the prophetic, studying scripture, mentoring prophets, and addressing the unique challenges faced by those who walk in this sacred calling.

As an experienced prophetic minister, Andrew combines biblical wisdom with practical guidance to help others navigate the complexities of prophetic ministry with integrity and purpose. Known for his out-of-the-box understanding and communication, Andrew has become a trusted prophetic voice in the body of Christ.

Andrew is a son of God, a husband to Roberta, and a father to three children with one on the way. He has also dedicated his life to equipping the body of Christ and advancing God's kingdom, one prophetic word at a time.

Web: www.righteousprophet.com
Instagram: @acphinney
Facebook: www.facebook.com/aphinney28

www.ingramcontent.com/pod-product-compliance
Lightning Source LLC
LaVergne TN
LVHW052026080426
835513LV00018B/2186